75
Cage-Rattling
Questions
to Change
the way
you work.

SHAKE-EM-UP QUESTIONS
TO OPEN MEETINGS,
IGNITE DISCUSSION,
AND SPARK CREATIVITY

Dick Whitney   Melissa Giovagnoli

McGraw-Hill

T. Auckland   Bogotá
exico City   Milan
Singapore
o

D0950575

Library of Congress Cataloging-in-Publication Data

75 cage-rattling questions : shake-em-up questions to open meetings, ignite discussion, and spark creativity / Dick Whitney, Melissa Giovagnoli.

    p. cm.

    ISBN 0-07-070019-2

    1. Corporate meetings—Miscellanea.   2. Public meetings—Miscellanea.   I. Giovagnoli, Melissa.   II. Title.

    HD2743.W526   1997

    658.4' 56—dc21   97-12468

                                           CIP

McGraw-Hill

*A Division of The **McGraw·Hill** Companies*

9 10 11 12 13 14 DOC/DOC 0 9 8 7 6 5 4

ISBN 0-07-070019-2

The sponsoring editor for this book was Richard Narramore, the editing supervisor was Fred Dahl, and the production supervisor was Tina Cameron. It was set in Frugal Sans by Inkwell Publishing Services.

Printed and bound by R. R. Donnelley and Sons Company.

 This book is printed on recycled, acid-free paper containing a minimum of 50% recycled de-inked fiber.

McGraw-Hill books are available at special quantity discounts to use as premiums and sales promotions, or for use in corporate training programs. For more information, please write to the Director of Special Sales, McGraw-Hill, Professional Publishing, Two Penn Plaza, New York, NY 10121-2298. Or contact your local bookstore.

Contents

36. What would your company be like if you had never worked there? *108*

37. On a typical day, which of the following takes up most of your time: a. dealing with difficult people; b. coming up with productive ideas; c. meetings that accomplish little; d. paperwork; e. using skills to achieve objectives? *112*

38. If you were to be fired or promoted, what would be the most likely reason? *115*

39. Which of these concepts—teamwork, learning organization, continuous improvement, leadership and quality—is the biggest joke at your company? *118*

40. What proverb captures the essence of your organization? *121*

41. How would Gene Siskel and Roger Ebert review your department's performance? *124*

42. If your company were a football team, what would be your strongest and weakest positions? *127*

43. What would appear bizarre, shocking, or amazing to a Martian visiting you at work? *132*

44. What would happen if your company instituted a one-year ban on meetings? *135*

45. What are the top ten reasons your people won't get the bonuses they deserve next year? *138*

46. What's your idea of a utopian workplace? *142*

47. How would the world's biggest cynic scorch your organization? *145*

48. Who would finally be able to solve your most stubborn work problem: a master psychologist, a venture capitalist, or an enforcer from the mob? *148*

49. You've just heard that all salaries, bonuses, and other compensation will now be based only on team

Introduction

> A good question is never answered. It is not a bolt
> to be tightened into place but a seed to be planted
> and to bear more seed toward the hope of green-
> ing the landscape of the idea.
>
> *John Ciardi*

Why are most organizations, departments, and individuals
unable to come up with breakthrough ideas or move in
new, unexpected directions? Is it because they're stupid?
Because they're uncreative? Because they're scared to try
something new?

We don't think so. Over the years, we've seen people
struggle mightily to be innovative and push boundaries.
They brainstorm in teams, they spend hours in quiet con-
templation, and they use various creativity devices to pop
that well-done idea out of the toaster. As part of this
process, they always ask the same questions:

- How can we reduce our costs?
- Is there a way we can better satisfy our customers?
- What can we do to facilitate better communication
  among our people?
- How can we use teams to increase productivity?

There's absolutely nothing wrong with these questions. But they generate answers that are obvious; they lead to strategies that are uninspired. For example, how can we reduce costs? By downsizing. We're oversimplifying, of course, but you get the point: Uninspired questions lead to uninspired answers.

Over the years, we've worked separately and together as consultants for a wide range of companies. During this time, we developed a process we refer to as "Questioneering.℠" It's a process designed to solve problems, generate fresh ideas and break down barriers; it's a process that's launched with a cage-rattling question. When you ask a group, "What would your organization be like if your mother were running it?," they think and talk about issues differently. The 75 cage-rattling questions in this book have been tested in the field, and we can report that they get people's minds and mouths moving in new and productive directions. They're outrageous, funny, provocative, disrespectful, bizarre, and dangerous. They are unlike any questions you've ever asked before.

You can use these questions in all sorts of ways. We've used them to facilitate idea-generating discussions; to help teams come up with breakthrough approaches to problems; they get individuals thinking in new ways about critical issues. You can use them for your own benefit when you find yourself doing the same old thing in the same old way.

It's interesting to note that these questions generate great discussions with all types of employees. CEOs respond as enthusiastically as the rank-and-file. The questions are as viable for addressing business strategy as they are for focusing on interpersonal conflicts. Any time you gather a group of people together to deal with a work problem, you'll be able to find a question here that will spark new thinking about that issue.

Without an off-the-wall book like this, people won't ask these questions. We want solutions as fast as possible and we tend to ask direct, specific questions designed to obtain targeted information quickly. Some employees—especially some managers—aren't trained to be reflective or idiosyncratic. They shy away from offbeat and controversial (and creative!) lines of inquiry. To them, Questioneering may seem like nothing more than a clever cognitive exercise.

But it's a lot more than that. Slowly but surely, businesspeople are beginning to understand the importance of out-of-the-box thinking, innovation, creativity, and the like. If you want to develop a breakthrough strategy, policy, product, or service, you had better begin by developing a different approach than your competitor's.

These quirky questions can help you do that. They give team members a chance to articulate a politically incorrect way to improve a process; they can offer a manager the opportunity to voice a radical idea about how to increase productivity.

Individuals and organizations need fresh ways to approach problems and opportunities. The 75 cage-rattling questions contained in this book will open your eyes to creative solutions you may have missed at first glance. Or they may give you the perspective necessary to create something that never existed before. Either way, they will shake you up and shake loose some terrific new ideas.

Dick Whitney
Melissa Giovagnoli

WHAT would your organization be like if your mother ran it

FIVE GREAT WAYS TO USE THIS QUESTION

- Helps people express what a company should do if it really cares about its employees; uses the symbolic figure of mother to communicate how a caring company should act.

- Produces a lot of common sense approaches to management ("mother knows best" ideas).

- Generates debate about a maternalistic versus a paternalistic organization, and female versus male management styles.

- When people express dissatisfaction with the way the company (or their team or department) is run, this question helps them think about a better way to run it.

- Relieves the tension when people are at each other's throats over important issues.

WAR STORY

A meeting at a small service firm had degenerated into bickering and name-calling. The firm had experienced a setback recently and there was a lot of hostility in the room. We'd been called in to help them analyze their problems, and this meeting was a kickoff to that effort. We'd started out matter-of-factly, asking for the reasons for the drop in revenue last year. Almost immediately, the ten staffers at the meeting began making accusations and second-guessing decisions. Arguments between individuals began breaking out like small brush fires; we'd try to put out one and another one would spring up.

Finally we asked our mother question.

"If it were my mother," one of the people said, "she'd send us all to our rooms if we didn't start behaving."

After the laughter subsided, another person volunteered, "My Mom would have never invested in the new computer system. She believed in paying cash up front for everything; she would have been horrified at the debt we incurred."

The tension eased and we received numerous ideas about how the company could be run better—or at least how it could be run with more humanity and common sense.

USER'S MANUAL

One of the interesting things about this question is that people's answers are hard to attack. It's one thing to tell Joe that his idea about expansion is baloney; it's another thing to say that his mother is full of hooey. Beyond the obvious humor attached to this question, it also has a civilizing influence on the discussion.

Perhaps the drawback is that people can get a bit carried away with their answers. We've seen some people go on and on describing their moms in all their glory (or all their horror—some people don't get along too well with their moms), or focusing on one specific thing their mom would do—she hates clutter, so she'd fire anyone who had a sloppy desk.

Follow-up questions are useful here if the discussion gets bogged down in how one mother would do one specific thing. To broaden the ideas, ask:

- How would your mother reduce costs?
- What would your mother do about policies pertaining to expense accounts and other perks?
- What managers would your mother approve of; disapprove of?
- What would your mother find frivolous about your company?
- What new product or service area would excite your mother the most?
- Would your mother solve problems through confrontation or consensus?
- Would your mother delegate decision making or would she centralize it?

Try this exercise if you need to propel the group beyond a discussion of trivial matters and on to substantive issues: Tell them that their mother has just been appointed CEO and has announced that five major changes will be made within the organization. Ask the group what those five changes will be.

What intangible BENEFIT makes your work worthwhile

FOUR GREAT WAYS TO USE THIS QUESTION

- Gives you a tool to identify your personal work values as opposed to the tangible benefits (money, retirement plans, promotions).

- Good tool to use when people aren't performing up to expectations; gets them to analyze whether the problem is that they're not enjoying what they're doing.

- A way for HR to better structure nonmonetary rewards; some people may respond to incentives such as a chance to work with peers on self-directed teams or recognition from a superior.

- A good discussion point when people complain about lack of suitable financial compensation; the question gets people talking about issues such as personal satisfaction, challenge, and growth as other forms of compensation.

A few days after a session with salespeople who worked for a major retailer, one of the individuals who had been there called us up and said he'd been thinking about our question. We remembered that during the meeting this young man had been very quiet, but now he seemed eager to share his thoughts. "When you asked us that question, it surprised me," he told us. "I've only been in the work-force for a few years since getting out of college, but I've had four jobs. The other ones I didn't particularly like, but this one I do. I always assumed that I liked this one because it pays better than the others, they're paying for me to take graduate courses at night, that sort of thing. But I thought about it and decided there was an intangible. It's that this place lets me be myself. All the other places I worked, I felt I had to put on an act. Here, they allow all of us to use our personalities to help make sales. The last store I worked at, they all wanted us to conform to this behavioral model. So the freedom to be myself, that's the intangible."

USER'S MANUAL

Some people do have to think about this question a bit before they answer. In fact, it's a good idea to be skeptical of quick and easy answers:

> What makes this job worthwhile is the people I work with.
> What's really important is having a boss I trust.
> The intangible benefit is that this is a place that encourages creativity and values everyone's ideas.

Here's something to keep in mind when asking this question (and when thinking about it yourself):

Real intangibles are often unique to the individual and can be illustrated by a story.

We all value different things. Some people love the responsibility their organizations give them; others thrive in highly structured environments. There are those who love to work in places that give them a sense of belonging and family; others derive great satisfaction from being recognized as innovators.

Whatever the intangible might be, each person should be able to relate an anecdote illustrating it. Encourage people to do so. Ask them things like, "Do you remember a time when you didn't have that intangible in a work situation?"

Sometimes it's best to give them time to consider the question by themselves. It really may be something they haven't thought about much, especially if they're young. We've even set aside parts of meetings when we've asked people to just sit and think about the question for 15 minutes or so before answering.

Here's another approach. If people are reluctant to say much or are offering easy and generalized answers, try asking one person to identify another person's intangible: "Ann, if you had to say what intangible makes work important for Jeff, what would it be?"

Finally, one last piece of advice: Be open-minded. Some intangibles may sound silly or trivial ("I want to work in a place that lets me sleep late and work late"). But in many cases, beneath the "silly" surface is an expression of an important personal value ("I want to work in a place that respects me as a human being").

3

If your COMPANY were to triple in size in five years, what event or idea might catalyze this SPECTACULAR growth **?**

THREE GREAT WAYS TO USE THIS QUESTION

- Fosters a growth mentality; gets people not only to think big, but to think about the factors behind bigness.

- A nice question for strategic planning or budgeting meetings; instead of planning for the next year or two with noses to the grindstone, this helps people plan with blue sky in mind.

- A good thought-starter for individuals; enables them to contemplate how they (or their department or team) might contribute to a company's growth.

WAR STORY

One group of executives of a high-tech firm tossed this question back and forth and finally reached consensus: Tripling their size in five years would result from the company going "virtual." They'd already taken small steps in that direction. Though it was a big leap to think of themselves as existing completely in cyberspace, it was feasible. They'd already downsized and outsourced to the point that the company required 50 percent less office space than it had two years ago. Though no one had ever seriously suggested that the company go virtual, the question allowed them to consider some of the ramifications. All sorts of ideas were generated about faster and more economic delivery of the company's software consulting services. Though it was impossible for the company to make this virtual jump in the next five years, it was feasible to do more via the Internet than they were currently doing, and if they could do it effectively, it would result in growth. Still, one financial executive clung to the notion of the totally virtual company, saying, "I know we can't do it in the foreseeable future, but think of how much we'd save in rent."

USER'S MANUAL

Here are the four most common responses to this question:

- acquisitions
- breakthrough product or service
- new technology
- brilliant leadership

To get the most out of this question, try to get people to map out a scenario based on their responses. For instance, if someone responds that acquisitions of Company X and Y will fuel growth, ask him or her to explain how: Will there be a synergistic mix of expertise; will the new hybrid company come out with great new products and services; will there be economies of scale; will they dominate a new market?

People really enjoy projecting how rapid growth might occur. Though much of what they say might be unfeasible, neat ideas often emerge that may have real-life applications.

Just as importantly, this question can help people analyze their own individual contributions to corporate growth. Ask the group to speculate how each of them might spur the growth they describe. What research, innovation, initiative, or decision might an individual make to fuel this growth?

4

What GAMES do you have to play to get on the side of PEOPLE who RIGHT matter in YOUR company **?**

THREE GREAT WAYS TO USE THIS QUESTION

- Reveals the politics that goes on in most organizations.
- Helps measure the extent to which politics impact decision making within an organization.
- A good way to determine the effect of politics on employee morale; helps determine whether it's common knowledge that to get a promotion, raise, bigger budget, or various perks you have to follow a political agenda.

WAR STORY

"The biggest game you have to play in this company is a literal game: Golf. No one moves up through the ranks unless they play it. And the ones who move fastest play it well."

When a guy made this admission during a meeting of middle managers at a small manufacturing company in the South, everyone chuckled. At first. Then they realized his response to this question was serious. He claimed the company's founder and his two sons, who now actively ran the company, were golf fanatics; that they routinely combined golf and business and expected others to follow their lead. The problem, according to the person answering our question, was that this game-playing excluded many of the company's minorities and women who didn't like or had never played golf.

This issue was later brought up to the sons of the company founder, who were the CEO and COO. They admitted that this was the case, but they said that it wasn't politics as much as business that motivated them to promote golfers. In their company and industry, a lot of deals were made on the greens. The two sons had always assumed that everyone understood this fact. As a result of our revelation, the company announced that any employee who wanted to learn to play golf would be given as many free lessons as he or she wanted.

USER'S MANUAL

Not everyone will be as forthright as the man in our war story. People are reluctant to talk about the games played in their organizations. To help them open up, guarantee anonymity. We sometimes share what we learn from this question with management, but we don't divulge the name of the person who gave us a particular answer.

Another way to get people thinking and talking is to offer them the following list of common political games and ask which ones are played in their company:

- Brownnosing—buttering someone up with flattery, tickets to popular events, etc.
- Backstabbing—spreading rumors or lies about a targeted individual.
- Stealing—taking credit for an idea or plan that was actually someone else's.
- Lobbying—currying favor with key people who aren't directly involved in a decision in order to influence the decision maker.
- Bribing—offering someone in a position of power an incentive to get you what you want.

Pretend your ORGANIZATION (or department) is an organized RELIGION. What are the core beliefs? What CONSTITUTES a sin?

THREE GREAT WAYS TO USE THIS QUESTION

- Stimulates a group to think and talk about the intangibles of an organization, such as values and culture; this is especially useful for a group of people who usually deal with the "hard" aspects of a company (accountants, MIS people, lawyers, etc.).

- Provides insights into your organization's soul.

- Helps identify needs of employees that aren't related to salaries and other tangible benefits—a good device to get people talking about what they really value in an organization.

At a law firm's partners' meeting, this question was discussed. One partner stated that the firm believed in the sanctity of the client relationship and worshiped the law. Another partner spoke eloquently about the firm's reputation as dealmakers and its belief in the tools of negotiation. A third partner made a strong case for dishonesty (not telling a client the truth) constituting a sin. Finally one of the older partners rose, shook his head, and said, "You fellows aren't working at the same place I am if you really think those are our beliefs. If this firm were a religion, we'd worship the almighty buck, and the biggest sin would be not to meet our quota of billable hours."

USER'S MANUAL

Expect a lot of malarkey at first. The war story demonstrates that this question gives people an opportunity to wax rhapsodic about the company's ideals. To get people down to earth and define the religion as it is rather than as they wish it might be, ask the following questions:

- What types of activities are most like rituals at your company (name anything from coffee breaks to team meetings to crisis phone calls)?
- Describe the rituals: How did they start? Are they the province of one particular department, team, or office? What is your favorite ritual?
- What do the rituals connote? What do they say about what's important in your organization?
- List five core beliefs and give examples of each (some incident, event, or conversation that illustrates that belief).

- What's the worst sin someone can commit and what's an example of it? What is the punishment for committing that sin? (There has to be a punishment or it's not a sin.)

- Who is the most spiritually advanced leader in your organization and why? What sermon does he or she preach?

- What story might be found in your organizational bible? (If this question stumps people, ask them to repeat a story that everyone has heard, one that is told after-hours at bars or around the water cooler.)

- What might your religious leader say to try to convert an outsider to your religion? What arguments might this leader muster to convert a heathen?

6

Your organization's BEST customer just called and said she was giving all her BUSINESS to a competitor. What do YOU think her reason for the SWITCH might be**?**

FOUR GREAT WAYS TO USE THIS QUESTION

- Isolates product, service, and support weaknesses before they become big problems.

- Avoids "We should have done this" thinking when customers suddenly switch to competitors.

- Analyzes customer relationships realistically rather than optimistically.

- Stops people at a sales meeting from resting on their laurels and promotes thinking about the future.

A manufacturer of mechanical components had lost significant market share to offshore competitors over a five-year period. Their perception was that aggressive price cutting caused the drop. We were called in at this point and had them work through the dreaded losing-your-best-customer question. Their first response was that perhaps their best customer might go with a low-cost competitor. "Are your best customers really so cost-obsessed that they'd ignore all the great service you give them?" we probed. Well, they responded, their customer was concerned about costs, but they were actually more concerned about delivery and support. "If we ever let them down in those areas, then we'd be in trouble." Aha, we said. So perhaps it was possible that their loss of market share to offshore competitors had something to do with delivery and support problems? After some discussion, they admitted that was indeed possible, though the politically expedient answer was that price cutting was the culprit. Aha, again.

USER'S MANUAL

Expect yourself and others to answer this question with numbers and data. People will naturally point to falling sales and other statistics to explain why a great customer would leave them; it's less painful than addressing the critical underlying issues involving customer relationships.

To shift the focus from statistics to relationships, follow up the question with these queries:

- How would you describe your relationship with your top customers?

- Which of the following descriptions best describes those customers' perceptions of your role: a. ally and advisor; b. reliable vendor; c. maker of the part they need; d. a temporary supplier (until they find someone better)?

- What have you done this month to sustain and grow the relationship with your customer contact? What would happen if this contact were to leave? Have you established other solid relationships with the customer?

Once the group has answered these questions, suggest the following proactive steps that make it less likely they'll lose their best customers:

- **Be paranoid.** Think about who might have a vested interest in seeing your relationship with a key customer decline. Assume they're doing their best to pry that customer away from you. What can you do to control or limit the damage your archenemy (most likely a competitor) can do to the relationship?

- **Think like your customer.** Perhaps the best way to do this is to concentrate on this question: What are the needs and demands of your customer's customers? And then: How can you help her meet those needs and demands?

- **Analyze all the contact points.** Make a list of all the people at your organization who have significant contact with your best customer and place a plus (adds to the relationship) or minus (detracts from the relationship) next to each name. How might you change some of the minuses to pluses?

- **Plan beyond the transaction.** Most people let good customer relationships deteriorate because they only "come alive" when there's business to be transacted. What might be done for a customer when there's no business on the table?

7

If you could create a new, unique POSITION for YOURSELF in your organization, what would it be

FOUR GREAT WAYS TO USE THIS QUESTION

- Gives people a chance to identify what they should be doing rather than what their job description calls for them to do.

- Lets people dream; it's a fun, fulfilling, and career-enhancing opportunity to think about the jobs that would make people happiest.

- Prevents job complacency; once people imagine their perfect positions, they are alive to new ideas, opportunities, and possibilities.

- A good tool for HR and management to develop key people; gives them clues as to the direction that a career should take within an organization.

WAR STORY

Cindy had worked in insurance claims processing for 18 years, and though she didn't hate her job, she wasn't thrilled by it. She liked her boss and the company she worked for, but the job itself had become old. She'd talked to her boss and HR people about other possibilities but nothing excited her; she'd even gone to see a career counselor, who also didn't help much.

Our question, however, got her thinking. She wrote out a new job description that really excited her; it entailed more planning responsibility, more involvement with designing claims processing software, and more travel (to benchmark other processing systems in other offices around the country).

Unfortunately, the job Cindy created didn't exist in her company. She talked with her boss about creating such a position, but he couldn't do anything. As much as he admired her initiative, he said that there were budgetary and other constraints that prevented that dream position from happening.

About seven months later, Cindy's company was acquired. She was reading the acquiring company's internal newsletter when she came across a position that sounded almost exactly like the one she'd constructed. Two months later, she found herself in her ideal new job.

USER'S MANUAL

While most people love this question and are energized by it, a distinct minority will look at you like you're crazy for asking it and say:

What do you mean, "new position"? I like the one I have now just fine.

For some, it's threatening to consider a new job within the company that doesn't currently exist. It's almost as if people consider it a trick question; it implies you don't like your current job.

If you sense that someone feels threatened, preface the question by explaining that no one has a dream job; that there are always things that could be better. If necessary, rephrase the question along these lines:

If you could add specific roles and responsibilities to your current job to make it better (and eliminate the ones you don't like), what would they be?

Another way to generate thought and discussion about this question is to feed people follow-up questions that allow them to imagine many possibilities rather than responding with something easy like, "Well, I guess I'd structure the job so I'd have more responsibility and have a chance to develop certain skills."

Here are some follow-up questions that will stimulate discussion:

- What would be your new title?
- Would you change the hours you work?
- Would you travel more?
- Would you need to go back to school or receive special training to do this new job well?
- What sort of salary, perks, and other compensation would you expect for this job?
- After doing this job for a few years, what would be your most marketable new skill?

8

What ARE the most popular lies people tell AT WORK

FOUR GREAT WAYS TO USE THIS QUESTION

- A barometer for the honesty (or lack thereof) of a work environment.

- Facilitates a discussion of the types of lies people feel compelled to tell to get their jobs done; leads to suggestions for alternatives to lying

- Creates awareness that lying is a negative form of communication, especially in sales, one that may result in short-term customer gains but long-term customer relationship breakdowns.

- Opens people's eyes to the pressures put on employees; alerts management to areas where they can help relieve those pressures and the corresponding urge to lie.

WAR STORY

Middle managers at a pharmaceutical company were debating this question. At first they were very indignant at the suggestion that lying happened frequently in their workplace. After a little prodding, however, they admitted the little lies; how they fudged a bit on when they'd finish a project, or why they didn't go to a company social function, or how they played golf on a "sick day." From there they talked about the lies between their salespeople and customers (telling customers a shipment would go out Friday when the salespeople knew perfectly well it wouldn't leave until the following Monday); how they sometimes were "forced" to lie to the media when a particular drug was the subject of a secret FDA report. They also discussed the lies between employees to avoid confrontation and conflict ("No one tells Mark that he's being unreasonable because no one wants to get on his bad side").

By the end of the discussion, everyone was astonished at how pervasive lying was. Even more revealing, just about everyone in the room agreed that most of the lies were unnecessary; that they were told because they were "quicker" ways of resolving an issue or they avoided emotional upset. With hindsight, it seems that the truth could have been told without any major negative impact. The group also related what happened in the few instances when a lie had been discovered—how it created distrust and soured relationships.

Though we're sure some of the people in the group continued to lie at work, we're also convinced that most now think long and hard about the consequences before telling another lie.

Lies exist in every workplace. Don't accept the statement that "no one lies here." Not only will this statement effectively end discussion of this question, but it is also a lie. A certain amount of lying is probably necessary in every company. You can't call an employee who is a moron "a moron." You can't tell a customer his request is imbecilic. You are forced to lie when the boss asks you what you thought of his speech, puffing out his chest in anticipation of your praise.

We've found that people can experience breakthrough ideas about workplace communication when they grapple with the lies they've heard and told. Encourage people to tell the truth about lies by:

- **Asking them to start with the little white lies.** These are the easiest ones to admit to. Once they're out in the open, ask everyone to address why these little lies are told.

- **Suggesting they examine a particular category of lies.** You might want to throw out some categories such as lies between the company and its customers; lies told to the media; lies between supervisors and subordinates.

- **Helping them imagine what corporate life would be like if everyone told the unstinting truth.** What would they tell their bosses? What would they tell their customers?

Ultimately, the best discussions of this question center on business relationships, the need for trust between people, and why honesty really is the best policy (within reason). You want a group to talk about things they might do to be more truthful with others without being hurtful or hurting themselves. If they don't bring this point up naturally, suggest it.

9

Think about a DECISION you or YOUR team are facing and ask yourself five CONNECTED "why's" (e.g., why should I open an office in New York; why am I RELUCTANT to do so ..).

TWO GREAT WAYS TO USE THIS QUESTION

- Helps you and others get beyond shallow thinking processes that fail to explore issues in depth.

- A great catalyst for groups to explore possible negatives surrounding an issue; overcomes people's reluctance to voice negative opinions because they don't want to hurt someone's feelings or appear to be naysayers.

We had a discussion recently with executives of a company who told us that they planned to launch a TQM initiative. Here was a great opportunity for them to ask themselves the five Whys. Their first why (Why are we doing TQM?): "Because everyone in our industry is doing it." The second why (Why will that cause us problems?): "Because competitors may improve their quality to the point that they approach our market-leading standard." The third why (Why can't we just keep improving our quality as we've done successfully in the past and keep ahead of competitors?): "Because TQM is almost magical in its ability to improve quality." The fourth why (Why do we say that?): "Because that's what all the articles, speakers, and books tell us." The fifth why (Why don't we do some research and benchmarking before we make the large investment TQM requires?): "Why not?"

USER'S MANUAL

You may find that you or your people feel more comfortable answering this question if there's a more formal way to do so. Some people don't like the open-endedness of the question and have difficulty understanding the point.

The point is that we make decisions for all sorts of weird reasons, and this question helps identify the weird ones. Specifically, people make decisions for three types of reasons, and two of those types confuse the issue and cause us to make the wrong decisions or to be indecisive.

Reasons for making decisions:

- Business reasons—the logic and economics of the business case.

- Personal reasons—likes, dislikes, family, etc.
- Political reasons—the possibility of getting a promotion, stopping a rival from achieving a goal, preventing a policy that will be harmful to you or your group, etc.

The following matrix will help you determine what reasons attach to each of your why's.

The Why Matrix

Why	Business	Personal	Political

Let's assume that the decision in question is whether a company should open an office in New York. The manager responsible for making that decision might complete the first why of the matrix as follows:

Why	Business	Personal	Political
Why should I open an office in New York?	It would add prestige and local sales presence.	I really don't like the place.	It might mean a promotion.
Why am I reluctant to do so?			
Why have I rejected the recommendation of the committee?			
Why did the committee recommend it?			
Why did this issue come up in the first place?			

10

What department do you find TO BE irrational, deranged, and in need of INTENSIVE group therapy

TWO GREAT WAYS TO USE THIS QUESTION

- Brings interdepartmental tensions out into the open; enables people to articulate why a particular department drives them crazy.

- Identifies departments that really may be driving everyone crazy with their insane policies and procedures.

WAR STORY

Everyone in the room was using the question as a spring-board to pounce on Human Resources. "They always tell us what we can't do, never what we can do," complained one manager from an accounting firm. "I have to do more paperwork because of those people; they're just covering their butts," said another. The complaints revolved around how HR frequently hamstrung hiring and firing efforts with quibbles and concerns that seemed irrational. To respond to those complaints, we brought in an HR supervisor who spent an hour clearly and carefully explaining the method behind the apparent madness of the procedures. The people in the room were ready to listen to the HR representative because of the question. Because they didn't interrupt, jump to conclusions, or tune him out, they left the meeting with a much better understanding of another function.

USER'S MANUAL

Cross-functional tensions aren't easy to remedy, and this question isn't a panacea. Still, it does get a dialogue going about the problem. We've found it helps a lot to bring a representative from the despised function into the room, but only after people have spewed their invectives.

This question fosters better understanding of other functions only when people are willing to open their minds. A lot of anger and frustration have to be put aside to listen to the other side of the story. Many employees have deep-rooted prejudices against other functions.

The point is to allow some fresh ideas about that function to take root. The best way to do that is to explain what seem like irrational and crazy policies. Either have someone from that function in the room, or play devil's advocate yourself to draw out the other side of the story.

What drives your customer's best CUSTOMERS crazy and what makes them EXCEEDINGLY happy?

FIVE GREAT WAYS TO USE THIS QUESTION

- Goes beyond the cliche of being customer-driven and gives your company a competitive edge.

- Increases market vision by focusing on what drives the strategy of your key customer (rather than what drives your own strategy).

- A tool to get people's attention during sales meetings; when no one can answer the question correctly, it energizes people to talk about what they really know about their customers' needs.

- A starting point for a discussion of new products and services that might benefit a key customer.

- A networking device that helps people look beyond the first line of logical customers for leads and contacts.

WAR STORY

Harold, the head of marketing and sales for a components manufacturer, was down in the dumps. Business was flat, the CFO had extracted all the cost he could out of the operation, and the CEO was expecting Harold's marketing and sales efforts to save the day. Harold, however, had just heard from his largest customer that next year's orders would be reduced because the customer's customers were experiencing tough times and sales were down.

This naturally prompted us to ask him the customer's customer question. Harold thought about it a minute and then admitted he didn't know. A little research, however, gave him the answers. What drove his best customer's customers crazy was lowball pricing by foreign competition; what would make them exceedingly happy would be an alliance with a reputable foreign manufacturer. It happened that Harold had a contact who helped cement a foreign deal for the customer's best customer. The following year, there was a ripple effect that translated into increased rather than decreased sales for Harold's company.

USER'S MANUAL

It's unusual for anyone in a roomful of people to know the answer to either part of this question. That's fine. The purpose of the question is to let people speculate about how they might find the answers. You might even want to take a break to do some research to see what they can learn, reconvening to review the results of their impromptu research.

Once people are able to supply ideas about what drives customers crazy and makes them happy, you need to ask another question:

- How can we help our best customer get rid of the thing that drives his customer nuts and supply the thing that brings a smile to his customer's face?

This question doesn't always have an easy answer. If what drives a customer's customer crazy is fluctuations in the economy, you don't have the power to do much about it. The goal of this question isn't always to solve your customer's customer's problem; it's to get you thinking about your customer from a broader perspective. The result may be a small thing: It gives you the chance to send a customer an article about the economy that he can pass on to his customer. Small things count. At the very least, it communicates to your customer that you care about his problems.

You (or your department) are UNDER an evil spell cast by a WITCH; who is the witch, what is the spell, and what words were UTTERED to cast it ?

THREE GREAT WAYS TO USE THIS QUESTION

- Gives people the chance to talk about feelings of helplessness when things are going badly.

- Helps people to strip the mystery from a run of bad luck and to figure out what's really causing it.

- An opportunity for people to exorcise demons and to feel that they have some spell-making power of their own.

Once upon a time (how else could we start a story related to this question), a cross-functional team got together to discuss all the screw-ups that had taken place in the past year. We were there to help them identify why they had missed deadlines and made mistakes that had prevented them from reaching their objectives. We weren't getting anywhere until we asked this question. When we did, most of the team members agreed that "James" was the witch. James had been a member of the team until they asked him to resign about a year ago; he'd been disruptive and divisive, and everyone was glad to see him move on. Still, when he left he was angry and at his last team meeting told them that "You'll miss me more than you know; when I'm gone you won't have me to blame when things go wrong."

His words had been prophetic. It wasn't that the team believed they were under a spell cast by James. Yet as irrational as it was, the team's problems could be traced to James' departure. This led us to focus on the timing: What happened around that time? After some discussion, we determined that the team's budget was reduced slightly at that time, another team member left the company, and the team was asked to take on an additional assignment from a recently disbanded team. None of these events, in and of themselves, hurt the team significantly. But taken as a whole, they had a substantial impact.

Recognizing this fact, the team felt better about themselves and now had specific issues they could address to improve their performance.

Expect people to place bosses, top executives, customers, regulatory agencies, and suppliers in the witch's role. Expect the spell's magic words to be along the lines of: "Your budget is cut in half"; "You'll have to get by with fewer people"; "There won't be any bonuses this year"; "You have to do twice as much in half the time."

We've found that people love this question when things are going badly and don't know how to answer it when things are going well. Obviously, it's best used when an individual or a team has had a string of bad fortune.

When people are finished casting their witches and spells and have had fun doing so, the key is to "dispell" the spell. In other words, what rational explanation is there for all the bad things that have happened? Encourage a discussion about why bad things happen to good employees. You want to move the discussion from fantasy to reality by probing for the real causes of downturns, missed deadlines, conflict, and so on.

13

What would your company's EPITAPH be if it went under TOMORROW

FIVE GREAT WAYS TO USE THIS QUESTION

- Cuts through all the corporate propaganda and really gets to the heart of what an organization is all about.

- Stimulates discussion in a meeting that is focusing on peripheral rather than core issues.

- A tool to gain insight into how others view the company.

- A dramatic device to alert management that something is seriously wrong with the organization.

- Gets people to articulate their worst fears about the company's future; it's a great device for a strategic planning session.

It was supposed to be a brainstorming session, but it felt more like braindrizzling. As facilitators of a group trying to evaluate some new R&D product ideas, we were disappointed with the shallow comments and uninspired analysis we were receiving. It seemed as if someone had taken the caffeine out of the coffee.

So we floated our epitaph question. It took everyone by surprise at first, and the first person who spoke offered a facetious answer. But then someone said: "It would be: 'We couldn't get an innovative product to market before the other guy.'"

Not everyone agreed with this epitaph. And that was terrific. Suddenly, the meeting came alive as the team members debated whether they were quick to market. Then they turned their attention to the R&D research and did a great job analyzing which potential product was worth rushing to market.

This question invites pithy responses, which are fine if they're also serious responses. What you want to avoid are frivolous epitaphs that bear no relation to an organization's real issues or vague ones that are too generalized to learn much from. For instance:

- We wouldn't be bankrupt if we gave John the promotion he deserved.
- Spent too much, saved too little.
- Didn't meet objectives.

Epitaphs are serious stuff, so you need to think about them seriously. The very idea of this question gets people to take a long, hard look at the essence of an organization. The brevity of an epitaph forces people to distill their feelings and thoughts into a crystal-clear sentence. When writing or speaking your company's epitaph (or asking others to do so), try to suspend your disbelief—convince yourself that your company has just gone under. If you do so, you'll bring to life a bottom-line assessment of the corporate spirit. Here are some good epitaphs we've encountered:

- A focus on the short term, an inability to see distances; the company died of a lack of vision.
- When it came to making an important decision quickly, we considered all the alternatives that existed (and some that didn't).
- We believed in putting our values before profits.
- Let no man say we never reengineered.

Suppose you're running a group, everyone suggests an epitaph, and then you're not sure where to take it from there. If a natural discussion doesn't flow from articulating the epitaphs, try this more formal approach:

- Ask everyone to relate the epitaph to a real problem that is currently hurting the company.
- Talk about whether there's a common thread to the epitaphs. Where do they conflict? Is it possible to construct one paradigmatic epitaph that encompasses the main points of all of them?
- Compare the epitaphs to:
  - The company's mission statement
  - The Chairman and CEO's letter to shareholders in the annual report

- The core positioning in your promotional literature and letters
- Customer satisfaction surveys you've accumulated
- Perceived reasons you've won and lost major business in the past three years

What is the most LIKELY reason SOMEONE would want TO JOIN your COMPANY; what is the most likely reason someone WOULD leave it **?**

THREE GREAT WAYS TO USE THIS QUESTION

- Probes deeper issues about what's attractive and unattractive about a company's culture; gives people the chance to express these opinions based on who has been hired recently and who has departed.

- Sets off fireworks about hiring and firing policies; gets everyone animatedly defending and assailing these policies.

- A good question for addressing troubling issues such as turnover and absenteeism; promotes creative thinking about ways to address these issues.

WAR STORY

This question was perfect for a group of senior consultants at a management consulting firm. They'd been having problems with a few clients who felt their thinking had a "sameness" to it. One of the clients claimed they had hired the firm for fresh approaches but they were just coming up with "tired old ideas." Or, as the client bluntly put it, "If we wanted ordinary strategies, we'd just assign these projects to our own people."

When we asked this question on a whim (we weren't quite certain if it would lead in an appropriate direction), we struck pay dirt. The group agreed that most people left because they were overworked and bored; they also agreed that they were attracted to the firm because it seemed like a challenging and glamourous work life.

What happened in between? The problem, most of them maintained, was that their clients all had the same, unsolvable problems—how do we operate leaner, how to reengineer without downsizing, how to become a global company. Every client engagement began to have the same feel, the same issues. Because most of the consultants had similar backgrounds—they'd all come from a handful of prestigious MBA programs—their thinking was very similar.

As the group talked, they came to the conclusion that it would really help if the firm developed a new process for working with clients, a process that would stimulate new (if somewhat riskier) ways of grappling with client problems. They also suggested that it would be beneficial to hire some non-MBA types who might contribute to a new process.

USER'S MANUAL

The caution we issue to every facilitator asking this question is: Use both parts of it together.

The dynamic of the question requires that people think about both why people leave and why people want to join. There's usually dissonance between the two, and the dissonance produces neat ideas and lively discussions.

You can tweak this question for use in different situations. For instance:

- Why did you join the company; why might you want to leave it? (This personalizes the question if the discussion isn't going anywhere when the focus is on others; good for an individual to use on his or her own as a thought starter.)

- Why did Jack leave the organization; why did Mary just join it? (By substituting names of real people, you give the question specificity that takes it out of the theoretical and anchors it in real employees.)

- Who do you think might leave the company in the next year; what type of people do you think will join the organization? (This is a good discussion tool for HR; helps them figure out the type of employee they're attracting and repelling.)

15

If your CRYSTAL BALL told you that most of the PRODUCTS or services you work with will be OBSOLETE in FIVE years, how would you react **?**

THREE GREAT WAYS TO USE THIS QUESTION

- Attacks the "everything's fine" mentality and gets people to look at harsh realities.

- A contingency planning tool; gets people to look at worst-case scenarios and create alternatives for if and when they occur.

- Brings organizational issues down to a personal or career level; allows people to link the organization's goals to their own professional ones.

WAR STORY

This question caused a great deal of commotion when we asked it in a room filled with R&D and product design people at a large organization. "I'd slit my wrists," one fellow said. "I'd start looking for a new job right away," another asserted. Everyone was highly agitated and pessimistic. Everyone, that is, except a senior guy sitting in the corner puffing on an unlit pipe (due to the no-smoking policy). He looked at everyone and said, "You know what I'd do if I heard that our products and services were going to be outdated in five years? I'd say, 'So what else is new?' Technological advances are coming so fast, I'd be shocked if they weren't outdated, and I'd suggest that everyone in this room better get used to that idea." Out of this discussion, a small committee was formed whose sole purpose was to examine products for signs of obsolescence on a quarterly basis.

USER'S MANUAL

Some of the best discussions occur when the spotlighted product or service in this question is one of the organization's most successful. When people are asked to imagine what would happen if the company's most successful product or service became hopelessly out of date, verbal sparks fly. Inevitably, some people take the position that this could never happen ("People are always going to buy our typewriters") while others can easily imagine how it might happen.

The point is to direct the discussion toward products and services that are currently state-of-the-art rather than ones that have already become ho-hum.

Expect some skeptical responses to this question. Some people will adamantly maintain that hot products and services will never go out of style. At this point, remind them of the following list of popular things that are no longer so popular:

- Atari home video games and Apple personal computers
- home milk delivery
- station wagons
- 8-track stereos
- dictaphones
- dot matrix printers
- the slick rule

You can spark some cage-rattling ideas around this question during budget meetings when people talk about allocating money for a new plant or increasing the advertising budget or hiring a firm to do new product packaging. Everyone feels fine about spending the money on a profitable product or service. But people question whether the investment would be worthwhile if the product became outdated in five years. This question gets people thinking in these terms.

16

What do people in your
department
most about GRUMBLE
over lunch

THREE GREAT WAYS TO USE THIS QUESTION

- If you want to find out what bugs employees, bug the lunchroom.

- Puts employee complaints in direct, colloquial terms rather than the indirect, formal corporate-speak that characterizes other forums for complaints.

- Reveals the gossip, feuds, petty grievances, and other issues that management never hears about but that are vitally important to most employees.

WAR STORY

About eight ad agency employees (members of the media buying department) had a lot of fun with this question. In fact, they created a list of 14 items that included a "No-smoking policy on 24th floor"; "Mrs. Jorgenson walking around and looking in our offices like she's a spy"; "The crummy bonuses last year even though an industry publication reported that our CEO got a $100,000 raise"; "Zeke Wilkins, the account supervisor, constantly makes lewd comments."

The media department supervisor was so impressed when the group turned the list over to her (they didn't have to do so; they wanted to) that she posted it on the office bulletin board. After it was posted, Mrs. Jorgenson stopped spying, Mr. Wilkins stopped being lewd and crude, and the CEO might think twice before giving himself a good raise while others receive lousy bonuses.

USER'S MANUAL

Do something with the grumbles. Make a list of the complaints. Have everyone discuss remedies to the grievances. Suggest possible solutions: Is outsourcing a remedy to the burdensome workload? Might the organization provide spot bonuses in lieu of annual ones?

Complaining is an energy source. Do something with it. Don't let all that energy dissipate without any productive ideas emerging.

Here's an idea-generating tool: Have the group discuss whether their grumbles are the result of a person, a policy, or a process. People stop and think about this one. Is Mr. Jones making them grumble, or is it the company's policy against this or that, or is it a process that requires time-consuming procedures? Finding the source of the grumbles can go a long way toward eliminating them.

What would be the TOP TEN questions customers and suppliers WOULD ask about your ORGANIZATION

THREE GREAT WAYS TO USE THIS QUESTION

- Helps determine if the organization's concerns are in line with those of customers.

- Creates a proactive mindset; gets people thinking about the issues that might arise in the future.

- Promotes thinking about your business from an outside rather than an inside perspective; reminds everyone how easy it is to maintain an insular mind-set and the dangers therein.

WAR STORY

A sales team had gathered to talk about how they might improve customer relationships. During the meeting, which we were facilitating, they were discussing their image in the marketplace. One salesperson opined that beyond the company's well-known service capabilities, customers didn't really care much about anything else. We asked the team to list the top ten questions customers might ask. When they shared their lists with each other, they were astonished. Each list was completely different. They were staggered by all the things that customers might want to know about the company but were afraid, unable, or unwilling to ask.

USER'S MANUAL

How can we reduce the amount of money we spend on your products and services?

Be prepared for questions like the one above. Most people who work for your organization will assume that customers want this question answered more than any other. While cost may be a legitimate discussion issue, don't get bogged down by it. It almost goes without saying that customers, suppliers, and others are concerned about reducing costs. This question will lead you in all sorts of directions if you don't fixate on finances.

You probably should also expect questions along the lines of:

We don't really understand what you guys do; can you explain exactly what it is?

The notion of clarity pops up a lot on the top-ten list. People feel that outsiders don't understand the services and products provided, the marketplace positioning, the stance on various industry issues. This is an opportunity to think about the company with fresh clarity. See if everyone in the room can describe exactly what the company does in 25 words or less. Condensing is a great tool for clarifying vague thoughts.

Other things you can do with this top-ten list:

- Have a group debate each individual's list and vote for the one that seems closest to the mark.

- Have customers judge which top-ten list is closest to their real top ten list of questions.

- Use it for entertainment purposes at team or holiday parties (read some of the funniest questions people came up with or create a fictitious list of top ten "personal" questions customers might ask).

18

What's the most innovative PRACTICE, service, or product your organization has launched in THE PAST year AND WHAT catalyzed that innovation **?**

THREE GREAT WAYS TO USE THIS QUESTION

- Use it to capture lightning in a bottle; this is an opportunity to analyze how innovation happened, commit it to corporate memory, and use it to make innovation happen again.

- Provides a method to take a conceptual discussion about innovation and tie it to real activities in an organization.

- Pinpoints the real source of a great new product or service; many times the wrong people are deemed heroes or a process gets more credit than it deserves; this question provides an opportunity to give credit where credit is due.

WAR STORY

In response to this question, one group focused on a highly successful piece of software their company brought out about a year ago. It was fascinating to watch them "devolve" the product, tracing it back in time as if it were their family genealogy. They actually mapped the various people, processes, and events that contributed to the product's success. What had started out as a fairly simple exercise turned into a complex task. It became clear to everyone in the room that this innovation didn't just happen, that there was a clear (though intricate) progression from idea to product. As one person put it, "Somebody didn't just come up with a great idea one day. We found out that great, creative ideas are a result of lots of people, lots of research, and some luck."

USER'S MANUAL

People sometimes answer this question without much thought, attributing a great new product or service to a singular event or person. Usually, innovation has many sources. To help yourself or others identify the real path of innovation, do the exercise described in the war story. Have people create a map that traces the great product backward to its original source, including people, processes, and anything else that contributed to its becoming a reality.

Here's another exercise that's a lot of fun and gets people thinking about innovation in new ways. After they've named the most innovative product, service, or practice, ask them how they might improve upon it. What would make it even more successful?

Here are some follow-up questions you can use to expand people's thinking about what makes a truly innovative idea come to life:

- Why did you name the product, service, or practice what you did? What about the product do your customers value?
- What's the most unexpected thing about this innovation's success? What about it surprised everyone?
- How big a role did luck play in the innovation's success? Is it fair to say that luck was the most significant factor, or was it a relatively minor factor?
- Could another company have had the same success with the same innovative idea? What is it about another company's culture, policies, or people that might cause them to be more or less successful?

19

Is your organization a FERRARI, a Ford Taurus, or a VW BUG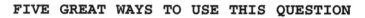

FIVE GREAT WAYS TO USE THIS QUESTION

- Analogies provide an unusual perspective that can start people thinking about organizations and teams in fresh ways—especially when you seem to have run out of new ideas.

- Useful for long-range planning and strategic brainstorming sessions; nothing gets the mental muscles moving like a debate over whether the organization is a Mercedes or an Edsel.

- Good communication and rapport-building technique for retreats and other situations when you want to start people talking to each other (everyone has an opinion about this question that's easy to voice).

- To release some tension and have some fun—you haven't lived until you've seen five grown men and women debating the merits of a Cadillac company versus a Miata firm or a green organization versus a blue one.

- Reveals a lot about an individual as well as about an organization; people's choices of colors and cars say a lot about who they are and what they consider important.

We were giving a talk to a group of sales and marketing executives when we posed this question. Though people at first thought it was a bit silly, they gradually got into the spirit as one person after another ventured opinions about their company's representative color and car. One person said, "Well, I suppose we're a four-wheel drive vehicle, since we're very aggressive in our pursuit of new markets and go where other companies can't." To which someone else in the room responded, "I'd say we're more like trucks, the way we roll over anything that gets in our way." Pretty soon people were defending their chosen vehicles with great passion.

USER'S MANUAL

This is one of those questions that often gets people going without much prompting. In fact, it often gets people in the mood to evaluate their organizations from a variety of other analogous perspectives. To facilitate this, offer the following questions:

- If your company were a famous building, what would it be?
- If you had to choose an object in the room that would come closest to representing your organization, what would you choose?
- If your organization were afflicted with a mental disorder, which one would it be (obsessive-compulsive, schizophrenia, panic attack, fear of heights, etc.)?
- If your corporation were a tool, what would it be?

CONSIDER the worst major
decision your COMPANY or
team has made in recent
YEARS; how did that
decision GET MADE: who
made it and why **?**

THREE GREAT WAYS TO USE THIS QUESTION

- Forces you to look at your decision-making process from a negative rather than a positive perspective (so you can learn from what you did wrong rather than just congratulate yourself for what you did right).

- A good tool to evaluate the decision makers. Who was involved and what did they do wrong? Who wasn't involved and why weren't they?

- A useful question for post-mortem analysis; helps people to figure out what might have been done differently in the decision making and to avoid making the same mistake again.

WAR STORY

The worst decision we made was to go global. Our CEO made it, and he did so because he's always been a sucker for trends.

It will come as no surprise that the person who made this statement no longer works for his company; he was one of a group of executives going through the outplacement process. When we asked the question, he answered with more than a little bitterness.

But his answer was useful. It stimulated debate about why all of them were out of jobs. In a way, it helped them go through a grieving process, examining why this bad thing happened, and why it happened to good people. People expressed anger at first, but after they got through the blaming they entered into a more objective discussion of what they needed to do to prepare themselves for workplace realities, and how they might make themselves so valuable that even if the CEO makes a boneheaded decision, they won't suffer because of it.

USER'S MANUAL

There's a lot of usable energy generated by this question. Bad decisions usually have bad consequences, and people naturally get worked up when discussing them—especially when they're asked who's to blame.

You'll also find people have no problem coming up with terrible decisions; sometimes what's hard is choosing the real stinker from a bunch of bad ones. It can also be difficult to isolate the reasons why the bad decision was made, since most people tend to develop distorted vision when they use hindsight.

To help you or a group of people figure out what went wrong in the decision-making process, choose from among these tools:

Rate each of the following three factors in terms of how much impact it had on the bad decision that was made (1 for large impact, 2 for medium impact, 3 for low or no impact):

- Personality: The person who made the decision always gets his or her way. _____

- Time: The decision needed to be made quickly and without benefit of sufficient research. _____

- System or process: The bad decision was a result of a system or process that was already in place (e.g., "We had to buy that awful software because it was the only program that would work with our computer system").

_____

- Trend-hopping: The decision was made in response to a feeling that something was "happening" and the company had better jump on board. _____

Here are some additional questions to ask:

- When a poor decision is made in your organization, what steps are taken to address it?

- What is your attitude about poor decisions you make: Do you tend to cover up the mistake or address it? Is your attitude toward bad decisions you make the same as your attitude toward bad decisions others make?

- What safeguards might your organization put in place to guard against poor decision making?

Tips for individuals and organizations are:

- **Individual.** If you're frustrated with your poor decision making, take Sigmund Freud's advice. He advocated flipping a coin and determining in advance what heads and tails will mean—heads means yes, you'll make the investment and tails means you won't. The point isn't that you have to accept the decision the coin dictates; it's that this action allows you to project how you feel about each decision. What happens when the coin comes up heads or tails? Were you rooting for heads or tails? Is your impulse to flip again? All this should tell you something about how you feel about a given decision.

- **Team.** Divide the team in half, having one group argue for the decision and create a written list of "pros." Have the other group argue against the decision and create a written list of "cons." Then have the groups reverse their roles and create new lists. Wait a few days and have the group discuss the lists they created. All this facilitates well-reasoned decision making in which emotion and personality take a back seat to logic and common sense.

21

What current management
fad has your company
adopted that is driving
you crazy**?**

THREE GREAT WAYS TO USE THIS QUESTION

- Stimulates discussion between management and employees about recently adopted policies and processes; a good way to get a "community meeting" started and get people's gripes out in the open.

- Gets people to stop griping and start exploring why a particular "fad" makes them nuts and to suggest ways that it might be modified to drive them a little less crazy.

- A way to avoid the employee sabotage and morale-lowering impact that occur when management fails to get employee input about new practices.

WAR STORY

One insurance company we worked with recently bought another insurance company. The acquired company was asked to switch from its old computer system to a new "hot" one used by the new parent company. The result was chaos. While the old system wasn't perfect, at least employees understood and could work with its imperfections. The new system had some advantages, but it also caused all sorts of problems because it was difficult for everyone to get the hang of it. Everyone was nervous about complaining openly about the system but privately they moaned and groaned, feeling that the only reason the parent company liked the system was that it was a hot system that lots of companies in their industry had started using. Our question helped bring this issue into the open, and management was shocked to realize the animosity that the new system was causing. While they haven't solved all the problems, now management and employees are at least talking about possible solutions.

USER'S MANUAL

Expect responses to this question along the lines of:

Our new _____ (policy, process, or practice) is stupid; the only reason we've adopted it is because _____ (name of executive) thinks it's on the cutting edge.

To use this question productively, you need to get beyond the complaint and open it up to objective analysis and discussion. To defuse some of the hostility, answer the following questions after stating what drives you crazy:

- Do you believe management's goal is to drive you crazy?

- Do you think senior executives sat down and tried to pick the one new policy or program that would drive you nuts?

- If you don't believe management is insane or sadistic, why do you think they adopted this awful fad?

- If management were to be candid about why they did so, what might they say?

- Can you think of any redeeming value of the fad? Is there any rationale that might exist for keeping it; is there anything that might be done to modify it and thereby make it more palatable?

Sometimes the problem is that management is so focused on taking care of the external customers that they neglect the internal ones. Employees see management as fad-fanciers because management hasn't taken the time to communicate the reasons for adopting a new program or policy. To open their eyes, try the following exercise:

- Create a fictional fad that is so absurd or outrageous that no one in their right minds would adopt it. Then try to create a rationale for it. Find an argument that justifies the financial investment as well as the chaos it might cause. For instance, the fad might be a new, politically correct policy in which employees are no longer allowed to use the male or female pronouns in memos and letters but are required to use an invented gender-neutral pronoun: "himmer." Defend this policy to the death. Do this exercise in a relaxed setting—a retreat or brainstorming session are good forums. Let management in on the idea behind the exercise and allow them to observe the interaction.

Is your organization (TEAM, boss) trying to rob you of your INDIVIDUALITY

THREE GREAT WAYS TO USE THIS QUESTION

- Addresses a growing concern among employees in companies that are moving toward a team-based structure; helps people talk about their fears.

- An appropriate question when the company enacts a policy (a dress code, stricter enforcement of hours) that makes people feel that the company wants them all to act and work in the same way.

- Spurs a philosophical debate about an organization's desire for people to work creatively and express themselves according to their own personalities; questions how much individual freedom the corporate culture allows.

WAR STORY

A new sales vice president had been hired at a consumer electronics company, and one of his first memos addressed the need for more paper documentation of leads, follow-up calls, status of prospects, and the like. The previous sales v.p. had had a much more laid-back attitude. Though there were paperwork requirements before, he didn't enforce them as long as people were producing.

We asked this question of a group of salespeople suspecting that the discussion would revolve around this memo. It started out that way but soon broadened out. The veteran salespeople complained not only about the new v.p. but about how the company's culture was changing. In the past, they maintained, management gave salespeople great freedom to operate as they wished. As long as they met their quotas, they were left alone. They felt the memo was just one indication that management wanted people to conform and "sell like little robots."

The group actually created a written list of ways management wanted them to conform, and they presented it to the new v.p. as well as to the CEO. While management didn't back away from their new policies, they were willing to open a dialogue about this issue that is still going on.

USER'S MANUAL

This question stirs people up. American workers, especially, treasure their independence. It probably has something to do with our heritage of rugged individualism.

While it's good to let people blow off steam every once in a while, this question may cause people to overreact. Our experience is that most managers and companies don't have any desire to rob employees of their individualism; there are usually good reasons behind policies that seem to be restrictive.

Once people begin talking about possible underlying reasons, the discussion becomes much more productive. Then a group can come up with constructive ideas about how to preserve individuality in the workplace and how management can better communicate the real intent of their policies. Lots of follow-up questions focus talk on the underlying issues, but probably the best one is:

- Imagine for a second that the policy or rule you hate wasn't designed to turn you into a robot. What other reason might management have had for coming up with the policy?

23

What false or outdated ASSUMPTIONS do people operate under at work

THREE GREAT WAYS TO USE THIS QUESTION

- An eye-opening discussion starter for groups examining their work processes.

- Encourages individuals to examine their own personal work assumptions to see if they're still viable.

- Helps identify problems that might be sabotaging a new process or other new work initiative.

WAR STORY

Profitability wasn't improving for an automotive parts manufacturer. It was tough to pin down the cause since unprofitable and marginal performance couldn't be fixed on one product line or function. We were working with a small group assigned to the task of investigating the lackluster results of the past few years and coming up with a strategy for turning the trend around. At first we struggled. Our first few sessions were filled with a great deal of talk about the need to reengineer and rightsize, and about how the company should take steps to improve customer satisfaction. But none of it really struck a chord. There was no real, identifiable cause for the slow but steady decline in profits and no real solution to build a strategy around. Then we asked our question, and after some discussion, one of the group members said, "Look, I know that the rest of you don't want to admit this, and maybe some of you don't believe it, but I'll tell you something. It's been so long since we've had a really good year that I think a lot of us assume that this company will never make money."

It turned out that this assumption was pervasive; that it limited many employees' actions—their willingness to take risks and to explore new markets. As a result, the first strategic thrust was designed to turn around people's attitudes about the company's ability to prosper in the future.

USER'S MANUAL

"What do you mean by assumptions?"

Some people may not understand exactly what this question refers to. If so, give them the following list of common false and outdated assumptions:

- The company will always take care of me (I'll have a job for life).
- We're always going to be the market leader.
- We'll have that customer relationship forever.
- We're too small to worry about global competitors.
- Teams are for special projects only; we work better as individuals.

You can also facilitate discussion of this question by asking everyone to express opinions about a given assumption. Here are some questions that will help generate a good discussion:

- Is the assumption held by one individual or many employees?
- How did the assumption get started in the first place?
- Was the assumption valid years ago, but not now?
- What damage does the assumption do in terms of work performance?

Choose a BRILLIANT product or strategy implemented by a COMPETITOR. Why didn't we think of that?

THREE GREAT WAYS TO USE THIS QUESTION

- Helps people look at innovation from a personal perspective rather than a distanced, intellectual one.

- A reverse engineering approach to innovation; the question stimulates individuals and teams to take apart other people's innovations and figure out what made them happen.

- Helps individuals and organizations see what they're lacking when it comes to innovation; gives people an opportunity to ask for the resources, time, authority, or other tools they need to come up with innovative ideas.

This question really hit home with a marketing director whose counterpart at a competing company had just launched a daring advertising campaign that was the talk of the industry. She was defensive at first, responding to the question by saying that the competitor has a history of doing innovative advertising and her company has always taken a more conservative approach. After talking for a while, this marketing director admitted that it wasn't the company's conservative tradition that constrained her ideas as much as a combination of factors—an ad agency that tended not to take risks, a boss who frowned on anything he perceived to be "radical," pressure from distribution outlets to stick to price-and-benefit advertising, the marketing director's reluctance to confront these issues with higher-ups in the company. The upshot of this discussion was that the marketing director should prepare a position paper on the subject and tactfully but forcefully explain how the lack of innovative advertising was hurting market share.

Expect defensiveness. People will offer excuses buttressed by rationalization supported by complaints. This defensiveness is fine, as long as you do something with it. A lot of energy is generated by excuses and complaints; take advantage of it.

Here are some things you can do to take the question to a higher level:

- Ask people to focus on the advantages that another individual or organization possesses that allow them to be innovative.

- Suggest that everyone list five adjectives that describe innovation and then discuss which adjectives their company is missing.
- Ask people to speculate about how they might come up with an innovative idea at some point in the future before competitors can. What advantages might they have in terms of innovation that others lack?

You'll know you've got people clicking with this question when they stop being defensive and start identifying what they need to be really innovative. Look for responses such as:

- Our team really needs better communication with our R&D people if we're going to make any breakthroughs.
- I have to spend more time by myself just thinking. Without that space to think, I'm going to rely on the first idea that comes into my head.
- I know that John and Susan went to a special creativity training session that really helped them develop techniques for coming up with fresh concepts. I think our group could benefit from that type of training.

Many times the end result of this question is a desire to talk about new ideas; people really are energized to explore ways in which they can come up with creative solutions to tough problems. Take advantage of this desire with a synergy circle. If you've ever seen the television talk show *Politically Incorrect,* you know what this is: It's a collection of "guests" from very different walks of life—a doctor, a famous actor, a janitor, and a comedian talking about the government's foreign policy. You can create the same sort of discussion group by inviting unlikely guests to talk about business issues. Bring in a consumer of your company's products; ask a reporter who covers your industry to sit in; request that a professor from a local college join you; maybe a local comedian can also attend. The synergy of dissimilar people with clashing styles and backgrounds often produces new ways of looking at old issues.

If Hollywood made a movie based on your organization, what would be the plot? Which STARS would you cast as the heroes and the villains?

THREE GREAT WAYS TO USE THIS QUESTION

- Stops people from falling into the empty cliches of business language and forces them to discuss the company in dramatic terms.

- A fun way to get people excited and talking about topics that seem boring; instead of another endless meeting that's nothing more than navel-gazing, this question helps people explore topics such as leadership and cultural issues from a "glitzy" perspective.

- Your script may reveal needed characters and roles that can't be matched up with current individuals.

WAR STORY

"No doubt about it," said a relatively young manager with a growing and innovative market research firm, "the plot of our movie would be a kind of family drama. About two years ago, this firm was locked in a battle between the traditionalists and the young upstarts as to the direction we were going to go. Our CEO, who was the head of the young upstarts' movement, fought the old guard, which was headed by the then-current CEO. There you have the hero and the villain. The thing was, the old CEO had been the young CEO's mentor, so there was a lot of bad blood when he rebelled. Eventually, he sold his ideas to the board and helped oust the old CEO."

Though the group in the room spent some time debating who should play the hero and the villain, they also talked about the substantive issues raised by the Hollywood treatment of their company's story. One employee in the room suggested that the theme of their movie was the irony of change—that it can build a company while also destroying relationships. For the next hour, everyone really addressed the impact of change on their working lives, especially the impact on their relationships with bosses, mentors, and other employees.

USER'S MANUAL

The only problem you may encounter with this question is a lack of focus. People may become so wrapped up in discussing which famous actor is right for a part that they ignore the larger issues. These issues emerge naturally if you can give people a structure and logic to answer this question. To help you do so, here's an outline for script development:

Step 1. Determine what type of movie you want this to be. What theme best fits your organization's culture, image, business practices, and the personalities of its leadership?

Adventure

Mystery

Romance

Documentary

Musical

Now, name your movie.

Step 2. The Plot: Pick five to seven key sequences for the movie. Think about major initiatives, events your organization has undertaken or will kick off in the near future. Briefly describe those sequences. Ask for lots of participation from others. (Don't forget to name theme songs.)

Step 3. The Script

- Put the sequences in any order or run them simultaneously.
- Tie them together as logically as possible to make a story.
- Write the ending. How do you see this scenario turning out? (Where do you think the organization is headed?)

Step 4. The Characters: List all the main characters. Don't think of specific people in your organization yet.

What characters are really needed to make this story work? Briefly describe these characters with as much flair and gusto as you and the group can create.

Step 5. Casting Call: For each character, select an individual or individuals (Remember, real actors have to try out!) in your organization that best fit the part. If you can't find anyone to fit the part, specifically define the actor required.

Step 6. Promotion: Write an ad for your movie that tells people what they're going to see, why they must see it, and what rating you think the reviewers will give it. Look at the movie ad section of your newspaper and use all of that Hollywood language.

Step 7. Critique: Have the group summarize and critique their work: What can be learned from your movie? What events could have been avoided and how? What scenes could have been added that would make this a more positive movie? What catalyst would be needed to edit in possible changes? Name the sequel to your movie and briefly describe what we can expect to see.

26

You've been chosen TO TELL the CEO that his services will NO LONGER be needed; what would you say to him to help him UNDERSTAND why he's being let go?

FOUR GREAT WAYS TO USE THIS QUESTION

- Allows people to criticize the CEO's performance in a kind and considerate manner (the guy's getting the boot, after all); elicits a rational critique rather than irrational invective.

- Helps people understand what the CEO and other executives go through when they're forced to downsize employees; demonstrates that it's not an easy thing to do.

- Communicates that everyone is accountable for his or her performance.

- Works well with a group going through outplacement or objecting to performance reviews.

WAR STORY

A company had just rightsized 5 percent of its workforce and morale was low. We were meeting with different groups of employees to determine what their fears and concerns were. We began asking this question routinely because it seemed to make people more empathetic to management. One employee, for instance, started his remarks by telling the CEO that he was being fired because he had taken his eye off the ball and allowed profits to dip to the extent that lots of people had lost their jobs. "Now you're one of them," the employee said. Then his tone softened and he added, "This isn't easy for me to do, since you have a family too and will be out of work—it can't be easy getting a job at your salary. It's probably even more humiliating for a CEO to get fired, since the trade papers will all write about it and how you messed up. We wish we could keep you on, since you did a lot of good things when you first joined us and we kept hoping you'd do more good for the company. But you seemed to get caught up in the social scene, spending all that time attending charity functions and the like. Not that we have anything against charity, but your primary responsibility was to us, and you let us down."

USER'S MANUAL

Watch out for anger. Even though the question is designed to evoke kinder, gentler critiques, sometimes people are furious at the CEO, especially if a lot of their friends have been fired. You don't want people getting up and tearing into the CEO, saying things like, "You fool, did you think we'd keep you on forever with your salary?"

It helps to do role-playing with this question. In other words, designate an employee to act as CEO; have this person respond as the real, fired CEO might. This usually causes people to soften their comments and give more thought to what they say.

One of the most useful aspects of this question is that it reveals employee perceptions of the CEO. These perceptions are powerful; they affect everything from morale to productivity. Will employees follow the CEO to hell and back? Or do they view him or her as mediocre? Perceptions can be changed, and this is a good forum for soliciting suggestions on what a CEO might do to change perceptions.

If you came up with a
BRILLIANT idea, who or
what MIGHT prevent you
from implementing IT **?**

FOUR GREAT WAYS TO USE THIS QUESTION

- Helps people think about making the impossible possible; generates ideas about how to remove the frustrating obstacles that prevent creative ideas from being implemented.

- Obtains good suggestions for making the decision-making process more participatory; brings people into the working loop who often are out of the loop.

- If you want to hold a gripe session, this question will make it a lively one.

- A tool for organizations that want to get their people thinking intrapreneurially and innovatively.

Patty told us that she thought long and hard about this question. She was in the MIS department of a mid-sized company, and though she knew her boss valued her programming experience and skills, he never acted on any of her suggestions that were of consequence. There were times when she was convinced she had come up with terrific ideas that would greatly increase the company's ability to get the right information to the right people at the right time (a big problem in the company). But her boss would say things like, "That's a good idea, let me think about it" or "I'll bring it up at the next staff meeting." Nothing ever happened. For a while, she thought the problem was her boss. But she asked other people in the company this same question, and they all talked about the problems they had with getting an idea accepted and acted upon. Patty figured out that the big obstacle to ideas was not an individual but the company culture. While there was no easy solution to this problem, Patty at least felt better about herself and when a new CEO came in and asked for input from employees about problems facing the company, she articulated this one in great and convincing detail.

USER'S MANUAL

Expect to hear a lot of blaming and people saying they feel powerless. In organizational and real life, many people believe they're unappreciated and unable to get their points across. It's fine to let people express these feelings, but to maximize the power of the question, here are three tips:

1. Turn the negative responses into positives by asking:

- Who might bring visibility and leverage to your ideas besides your boss? Is there anyone who might be a good internal champion?

- What can you do to minimize the time and cost it would take to develop your idea?

- Can you partner with another organization or entity to get partial funding for your idea's development?

- Why is your idea so brilliant? How will it help do things faster, cheaper, more efficiently, with less complaining, etc.?

2. Focus on the obstacles rather than the brilliant idea.

- Identify whether the obstacle is a person, a process, time, money, the corporate culture, or some combination of these factors.

- Once the obstacle is identified, ask the group to reach consensus about whether there's a more significant obstacle. As our war story illustrates, the most obvious choice of an obstacle isn't always the right one.

3. Communicate to people that brilliant ideas marketed brilliantly within a company can often overcome obstacles, as demonstrated by the following story:

- Two employees at a large corporation had been doing research in two different areas. They put their heads together and came up with what they thought was a neat idea for a new product. Unfortunately, initial market surveys strongly indicated the product would fail. This might have killed the idea then and there, but these two men were convinced they had something, so convinced that they distributed their sample product to a variety of people inside their company. Everyone loved it, and 3M decided to take a risk and launch Post-It notes.

28

If you could trade work
SKILLS the way kids
swap baseball cards,
who would you trade
with and for what SKILLS

?

TWO GREAT WAYS TO USE THIS QUESTION

- Gets people to admit that they're not good at something and identify skills they need to learn.

- Helps an organization understand what skills employees feel are important for particular jobs.

WAR STORY

A salesperson at a large company responded to this question by saying she'd like to swap skills with the CEO. She said she could really use the CEO's superior networking skills to establish a larger prospect base, and the CEO could use her time management skills because she was always late for meetings, working weekends, and cancelling vacations.

When the salesperson said this, the CEO wasn't in the room; it's unlikely she would have said what she did if the CEO were there. When we were discussing the results of the meeting with the CEO and shared this story with her, however, the CEO nodded her head and said that she'd be willing to make that swap any day of the week. A short time later, the CEO arranged a lunch with this sales executive and they shared ideas about the particular skills they each wished they possessed. While the CEO and sales executive didn't instantly master each other's skills, they at least obtained some ideas about how to do so.

USER'S MANUAL

If people aren't sure what skills they want to acquire or trade, start out by asking everyone to identify the skill they consider most important to getting their job done. As participants verbalize skills, record them on a large piece of paper for everyone to see. Then ask which skill each individual would love to have. Very quickly, people will be bartering skills with each other.

Another way to make this question work is to pair people up and have them discuss a trade of skills. It's likely that each person will find some work trait in the other that he or she would like to have.

One of the things to watch for with this question is that everyone focuses on the skill to be acquired. There's also a lot to be learned from hearing skills people are willing to trade away—you may identify an area that training is focusing on that really isn't that important for a given job.

29

What would motivate you to work SEVEN days a week, twelve hours per day, for a month on an IMPORTANT project **?**

THREE GREAT WAYS TO USE THIS QUESTION

- Helps find people's motivational hot buttons; gives managers a sense of what really would drive subordinates to work extremely hard.

- Good starting point for a team discussion of productivity.

- A catalyst for analysis of a company's reward and recognition system; helps HR and others determine the financial and nonfinancial tools that really motivate people to work.

A group of line managers had just gone through a period in which they'd been working extremely hard, if not 70-hour weeks. They had monthly meetings to discuss issues of concern to all the line managers, and this question came up. While one or two people said "It would take a lot more money than they're paying me now," most of them focused on the involvement of upper-level managers as important. They said that they resented seeing executives waltz in at 9 a.m. when they'd already been working for two hours, and leave at 5 p.m. when they'd still be there for another two hours. They said they didn't resent it just because they had to work and the executive staff didn't, but because top managers had a lot of expertise that could help them complete projects faster. They added that they were motivated by the informal mentoring/ coaching system such executive involvement would create.

As a result of this discussion, a number of top-level executives volunteered their services to the line managers on the next work-intensive project.

USER'S MANUAL

You won't get many sizzling concepts out of a discussion that just focuses on money. Just about everyone is motivated by money, and it may be that people feel woefully underpaid when they're asked to work long hours. But there are lots of other things that can motivate people to work hard, and you want to move the discussion in these directions.

Try this three-step approach:

1. When group members respond that they feel crummy because they're underpaid, acknowledge that fact and ask what, besides money, might make them feel better.

2. Suggest a series of unusual "perks" that might motivate them: A drawing for a free trip anywhere in the world; a year of free Friday lunches for the team at the restaurant of their choice; career counseling services from an outside career coach; the CEO's involvement in the team's planning sessions; a trip to Vegas with a stake provided by the company.

3. Ask them to focus on a time when they worked harder than they ever had before. It doesn't have to be when they worked for their current company; it could have been with another employer or at a summer job or in school. Have them relate their experiences and explain how they felt at the time. When someone tells a story about working very hard and feeling great about it, concentrate on why the person felt so good. Ask the group how the company might help them replicate that situation.

What about work most REMINDS you of what you hated about SCHOOL

THREE GREAT WAYS TO USE THIS QUESTION

- Memories of a despised teacher or a boring class or a bully translate well to an organizational setting; provides a vehicle for people to communicate feelings about work that they might otherwise keep to themselves.

- It's instructive to hold up negative school experiences as a model to avoid at work; a way to identify pedantic bosses and stupid rules and regulations.

- The resulting discussion often demonstrates to managers that employees should not be treated like schoolchildren.

A division of a mid-sized direct marketing company was experiencing high turnover and no one could pinpoint the cause. We gathered a group of employees from this division in a conference room and began probing why their cohorts were leaving. At first we received the usual complaints: not enough money, the job is boring, other companies are offering more opportunities for advancement. All of these might have been valid reasons, but the group wasn't very vociferous in defending these reasons and they couldn't reach consensus about any one of them.

When we asked our question, however, the consensus was obvious. Everyone drew the parallel to a teacher who tells students everything they should do and doesn't respect their opinions or ideas. The head of the department, they claimed, gave them absolutely zero freedom to be innovative or even to vary from the routine format (the group designed direct-mail packages).

Though this discussion wasn't the only reason, the head of the department was transferred to a different facility where he could work more independently and wouldn't impose his strict classroom rules on another group.

The only difficulty we've encountered with this question is that groups sometimes become overly focused on negatives about work. If you're tired of hearing employee complaints and you want to elicit positive ideas, turn the question around as follows:

- What about work most reminds you of what you loved about school?

If people need a bit of prompting (which they might, since most employees probably can think of things they hated faster than things they loved), ask them if there is a supervisor who reminds them of a favorite teacher; if there's a work assignment that's like gym, art, or another popular subject; if they ever feel the way they did when they received an A on a test or were singled out for praise by a teacher.

Once you've identified the positive parallels, the discussion might flow around how more of those good feelings can be generated during an average workweek.

Your manager issues an order that ALL EMPLOYEES must listen to NEW AGE music for ten minutes at the start of each workday. Your MANAGER is convinced this will improve motivation and PRODUCTIVITY. How would you react ?

THREE GREAT WAYS TO USE THIS QUESTION

- A forum for employees to vent their frustration with bosses who give them seemingly silly, offbeat, or unproductive things to do.

- Fosters a discussion between managers and employees about a sensitive subject—the artifice of New Age music makes the subject less sensitive and easier to discuss.

- Prompts a discussion of real motivation versus artificial motivation.

WAR STORY

We asked this question during a meeting of customer service representatives employed by a large retailer. At management's behest, we were attempting to understand why this department's morale always seemed so low and why they didn't respond to employee incentive programs management had launched in the past year.

The question evoked knowing grins. As one person said, "We'd react to that New Age junk the same way we react to that program that awards us bonus points at the end of each month or the thing they tried last year, bringing in this motivational speaker who used to be a star athlete. We'd listen and pretend that it was a good thing, but we'd know it was just plain silliness."

Gradually, the discussion shifted from New Age music to what really would motivate them to work harder, longer, and more enthusiastically. One of the best insights was that many people in customer service viewed their jobs as stepping stones to other jobs with the retailer; many of them wanted to receive training to move into sales or the MIS group. What would really motivate them, they agreed, was the chance for people who performed well in customer service to receive that training.

USER'S MANUAL

Sometimes the most revealing activity is one that is absurd or unlikely. Most managers today don't "mandate," especially in the way described in this question. Yet most managers do issue memos, instructions, and advice, and the absurdity of this question allows people to be less uptight and defensive when talking about stupid motivational ploys.

You can expect a certain resentment from some employees in response to this question; to get beyond that you'll need to ask follow-up questions such as:

- Why do you automatically assume that New Age music won't have a positive motivational effect?
- Is there another type of music that might motivate you better?
- If there were a position like v.p. of motivation at your organization and you were appointed to it, what types of policies would you enact?

If you're using this question with managers, they may not take it seriously; they don't see the connection between their management style and mandating listening to this music. Try the following script:

Pretend that you passionately believe in the power of New Age music as a catalyst for introspection; that you've read studies and seen evidence that document its ability to help employees discover aspects of their work performance that they might otherwise miss. In fact, in a previous position your boss had you do this same exercise and you learned a great deal about your propensity for making quick decisions without much thought. You recognize that there are people in your group who will be skeptical about this New Age music concept, and that at least one person in the group will be resistant to the concept. Finally, many people in your group complained about their last performance reviews—they thought you were too tough on them. Their response to the performance reviews is a major reason why you decided to issue your New Age music edict.

Put yourself into this scenario and respond to the following:

- Imagine a memo you might write telling your group about your New Age music policy: e.g., when it will start, the purpose of it, how and when you expect them to listen to the music, resources they can use to get the most out of it, etc.

- Jump ahead a bit in time. Two people come into the office after receiving the memo. The first one is very upset. He says, "I just read your memo, and I have to tell you I'm very upset because _____" (complete sentence). The second one comes in a few minutes later and says, "I just read your memo, and what I really like about this concept is the way you _____" (complete sentence).

32

If someone BURST into your office and shouted, "I've got GOOD NEWS and bad news," what do you think those two pieces of news might BE **?**

TWO GREAT WAYS TO USE THIS QUESTION

- Encourages people to express their top-of-mind fears and hopes about their jobs, their teams, and their organizations.
- Opens up a department to a discussion of how things are *really* going.

WAR STORY

We used this question with a team that was under pressure to meet an ambitious deadline and objective and was frustrated by their slow progress. One person on the team responded to the question by saying, "Okay, our team sponsor comes rushing into my office and says, 'Sharon, I've got good news and bad news. The good news is I got a two-week extension on the project deadline for the team. The bad news is that if you don't deliver, you're all going to be fired.'"

When the team sponsor heard this story, he met with the team (after laughing heartily at what the team member said) and reassured them that they could have a deadline extension and that nothing catastrophic would befall them if they couldn't meet the objective in the extended time frame.

USER'S MANUAL

Though it wasn't our intention when we formulated this question, we've found that the good news and bad news people express are usually related in some way. There's nothing wrong with this, though sometimes it prompts people to respond facetiously rather than honestly; it's as if they see the question as an opening for a punch line.

To get them to take the question more seriously, here are some ideas:

- Tell them the good news and bad news *cannot* be related.
- Ask them to identify the messenger of good and bad tidings.
- Suggest they focus the good and bad news on a particular subject or category—careers, a team project, a change in management, a merger or acquisition, competitors, or a new policy.

You probably work with
one or two incompetent
or OBNOXIOUS people.
How do they manage to
keep their jobs

THREE GREAT WAYS TO USE THIS QUESTION

- A catalyst for human resources people to talk about their rewards and recognitions system.

- A way to "air out" personality conflicts by getting issues into the open.

- Lets people blow off steam and curse the world that allows corporate sociopaths and lazy bums to work at the company and make everyone else miserable.

WAR STORY

Jerry had more lives than a cat. By all rights, he should have been fired many times. A human resources manager whose mistakes had resulted in a few costly lawsuits and who took more two-hour lunches than anyone in the company's history, Jerry had survived for 14 years. During a cross-functional team meeting, our question brought out a lot of negative information about Jerry. Everyone agreed he was incompetent; his laziness was legend. Some people suggested that Jerry didn't start goofing off or screwing up until after he'd been with the company for seven or eight years, and his seniority kept him from being fired. Others speculated that despite his incompetence, Jerry was charming, and his charm had endeared him to certain executives. Though Jerry was the initial focus of the discussion, talk soon turned to others like Jerry who had managed to remain employed even though they should have been let go. The conclusion the team drew was that incompetent and obnoxious people can retain their jobs if they demonstrate a saving grace—in Jerry's case, it was charm. They also concluded that the system had to change and began working on a plan to change it.

USER'S MANUAL

If you want this question to lead to a gripe session, that's fine. It often happens that people respond with complaints about individuals who received promotions and raises (instead of themselves). There's nothing wrong with allowing people to expel some anger and frustration.

But if you want to move beyond gripes into more productive territory, turn the discussion from general gripes to specific complaints. For instance, ask what characterizes Mary's obnoxious personality. Does she:

- Spread nasty rumors about others?
- Take credit where credit isn't due?
- Never listen?
- Complain constantly?
- Butter up the boss?

Also, ask people to identify specific performance issues. If Jack is called incompetent, does he:

- Miss deadlines?
- Communicate poorly?
- Never come up with creative ideas?
- Fail to work well in teams?
- Spend more time covering his butt than working on a project?

After people specify their complaints, get them to justify firing the person because of them. This will cause everyone to test his or her own assumptions about what constitutes a "fireable" offense. After that, ask them to speculate as to why the organization has not fired these people.

The goal of all this is to have a broad-based, wideranging discussion in which people answer the question as follows:

"I can name seven or eight people in my department who are impossible to work with because they never get projects done on time or are just seriously disturbed individuals and don't know how to work with others in team settings. They get by because they know how to play this company's

game; they know who to butter up when they can't get away with their usual sloppy work and how to bend the rules and not get caught."

This is a great opportunity to begin a problem-solving discussion of these political issues.

34

What product, service, fUNCTION, department, or other component of your business WOULD you eliminate if you had to get rid of "dead WEIGHT"

THREE GREAT WAYS TO USE THIS QUESTION

- Identifies a company's weaknesses; by elimination, it also identifies a company's strengths.
- Generates debate among any group of employees (junior or senior, manager or rank-and-file) about who or what is no longer adding value.
- A tool to figure out what function might be outsourced.

WAR STORY

A group of salespeople from a mid-sized insurance company were gathered together by their supervisor for a brainstorming session. Their supervisor fed them this question on a whim, unsure as to how they would react.

He was surprised to see how vociferously they responded. The salespeople said that they knew this was a touchy subject, but since the supervisor had asked …

They began explaining how they felt they were trying to sell too many insurance products to customers. They understood the company's philosophy had always been "too much rather than too little" and that their advertising emphasized the wide range of available policies. But, they maintained, certain products were rarely sold and when they were, they generated relatively little revenue and a lot of paperwork.

As a result of the group's feedback, the company launched a study of its products to determine which ones were weak performers and should be eliminated.

USER'S MANUAL

We usually get a good response to this question without much prompting or follow-up questions. The only problem that sometimes surfaces is that the question touches a political nerve (as in the war story) and a group is reluctant to suggest eliminating the boss's favorite product or service or outsourcing a function run by someone with clout.

An easy way to make the question less threatening is to modify it as follows:

What product, service, function, department, or other component of your business isn't performing at the same level as all the others?

35

If your organization had the opportunity to make an ENORMOUSLY profitable move but would violate its principles in the process, what would it do

FOUR GREAT WAYS TO USE THIS QUESTION

- Forces people to confront the increasingly common clash between values and results; helps people consider not only what the organization would do, but what they would do themselves.

- Helps individuals and organizations define what their principles are and the relationship of principles to results.

- A discussion starter for people who are called upon to make these principles-versus-results decisions; good for managers, salespeople, marketing department employees, anyone who works closely with outside suppliers, etc.

- Helps management determine what principles in an organization are most likely to be violated.

WAR STORY

We remember the time we presented this question to a group of employees who worked in the purchasing department of a company. They were evenly split on the question; some argued that the company would always put profits ahead of principles, while the other group argued that they would only do so in rare situations. Eventually, the discussion turned (as it often does) to what each member of the group would do if placed in this difficult position. A common issue was what would happen if a supplier offered them a kickback or what might happen if they had a chance to get a great deal on a quantity of supplies that would really help the company, but in turn they had to violate the company's policy toward suppliers (by giving them preferential treatment when a contract was up for bidding, for instance).

Though there was no resolution to this question, the members of the group admitted that it helped to talk about what they and the organization might do when faced with these types of situations. As one of the purchasing employees put it, "If I really believe that my employer is going to stick to its principles, I think I'd be likely to stick to them too."

USER'S MANUAL

We've found that people tend to be evenly divided on this question, which helps spark debate. One goal of the question, however, is to get people to bring the debate down to what they would do if forced to choose between principles and profits.

To bring the discussion to an individual level, try to pose an ethical/profits dilemma relevant to participants' jobs. Here are some dilemmas you might want to use:

- **Lying:** You've been asked to lie to the media in order to cover up a sexual harassment episode in your department; you're told that if the story hits the media the wrong way, it will result in a downturn in the the company's stock and might trigger a downsizing.

- **Silence:** You know inferior parts are being used in the manufacture of a product but your boss tells you that everyone in your industry does it and that what the customers don't know won't hurt them.

- **Favoritism:** You're supposed to treat all vendors equally and openly, but you know of one particular vendor who is willing to cut corners and bend safety rules to get the job done fast; going with this vendor will help your group meet its deadline but it will also violate vendor policy.

36

What would your company
be like if you had
NEVER worked there **?**

FOUR GREAT WAYS TO USE THIS QUESTION

- Helps assess how employees feel about their contributions (or the lack thereof) to the organization—a great way for them to gain another perspective on their performance.

- Sparks debate and discussion in performance review meetings with subordinates or team members: Have you really made a difference to the organization?

- Helps people discover if they're "disconnected" and reconnects them to team or corporate goals. Rather than waiting for productivity decline, increased absenteeism, or other red flags, you can use this question to determine who is working more for themselves than for the organization.

- A tool to help people recognize how their day-to-day work impacts a larger process or group.

We used this question during a bank employees' training session, and it unearthed a wide range of personal fears such as "I don't feel like I belong yet" (this from someone who had been with the organization for three years); "The question makes me feel like I really haven't existed for the 14 months I've been here"; "If I had more technical training, I would feel more important"; "I'm not sure that anyone could do what I do."

By addressing these fears and discussing their root causes, we helped people to see: a. that their fears were unfounded and their work had made a significant contribution; b. that if they hadn't made much of an impact in the past, there were many opportunities to make an impact in the future.

Some of the positive responses we've received to this question include:

- We would never have reached our performance goal last quarter.

- (Name of employee) wouldn't be here because I helped him or her deal with some serious problems.

- A process (manufacturing, MIS, etc.) wouldn't run nearly as efficiently as it does.

If you or your people are cynical or embittered, you can probably expect some variation on the following answer:

If I had never worked here, the company would be exactly the same as it is now.

The positive responses are great and usually lead to a productive discussion not only of positive contributions in the past but ideas for contributing in the future. Encourage people to speculate about new and innovative ideas they have for helping their team, process, department, or organization work better.

Negative responses need a bit more imaginative facilitation. Try telling the group to do the following:

Imagine a worst-case scenario for your company (or team) if you had never worked there. What programs, policies, or processes might not exist or wouldn't run as smoothly? Which people wouldn't perform as well or would have left to work for some other organization? Take your answer to an extreme: What are the absolute worst possible scenarios, no matter how unlikely they might be? Is it possible that for lack of your efforts, the company might have come up short in a critical area? Might it have resulted in a significant loss of revenue? Might that in turn have resulted in a downsizing? Do your best to imagine the worst.

Here are some other tools to use if people respond negatively:

- On a scale of 1 to 5, rate your importance to the organization (5 means you're of crucial importance, 1 signifies you're of no importance at all).

- What would your company be like if _____ (name of your boss) had never worked there?

- How many hurdles are placed in front of you that prevent you from doing your job or achieving group goals? Name three of those hurdles.

- What's one thing you might do that would have a significant impact on the company? (Punching an obnoxious boss or destroying a recalcitrant vending machine are not acceptable answers.)

37

On a TYPICAL day, which of the following takes up MOST of your time: a. dealing with DIFFICULT people; b. coming up with productive ideas; c. meetings that ACCOMPLISH little; d. paperwork; e. using skills to achieve

OBJECTIVES

FOUR GREAT WAYS TO USE THIS QUESTION

- A vehicle a supervisor can use when people complain that they don't have enough time to complete an assignment.

- If teams find themselves stuck in the mud, this question sometimes reveals why they're stuck.

- Helps employees articulate the problems they're having with time management or, conversely, gives them the chance to discuss how they manage their time productively.

- Attacks the subtle hypocrisy that can pervade companies pretending to get a lot of meaningful work accomplished each day.

WAR STORY

We know of a CEO who liked this question so much that he asked it when he was giving a speech to the company's entire salesforce. He asked for a show of hands when he read A, B, C, D, and E, and as he expected, the majority raised their hands for the positive B and E responses.

He then went around the room and randomly picked people, asking them to tell him if they had attended any meetings the previous day; if they had spent any time on paperwork; if they had been involved in working out personality conflicts between others or in direct arguments with supervisors, subordinates, or peers.

One after the next, they related stories of meetings, paperwork, and dealing with difficult people. When they were finished, the CEO gave everyone a big smile and offered his congratulations for everyone's willingness to work twelve-hour days, six days a week. For a moment, everyone was confused by what seemed to be a non sequitur. But then the CEO added, "I'm sure all of you must be working that long and hard, since you couldn't be spending most of your time coming up with ideas and meeting objectives if you're also doing all that other stuff."

USER'S MANUAL

As our war story illustrates, people will initially respond with letters B and E, especially if their supervisors are in the room (or if they expect them to be privy to their responses). If this happens, you can do as our war story CEO did and question people about what they did the previous day.

Another idea is to focus on the positive responses and probe: "What skill did you use to achieve that objective?"; "What idea did you come up with?" The odds are that people will stutter, stammer, and eventually admit they didn't accomplish as much as they had hoped.

The best discussions around this question, however, develop when people volunteer ideas about how to reduce the time they spend in worthless meetings, filling out paperwork, and dealing with difficult people. To facilitate these discussions, ask people for alternatives:

- What alternative was there to having that three-hour meeting on Wednesday?

- Is there another, less time-consuming way to resolve the conflicts that break out between Mary and Steven every week?

- If the IRS can come up with a short tax form, isn't there a way we can reduce the performance review form by 50 percent?

If you were to be
fired or promoted,
what would be the most
likely REASON

?

THREE GREAT WAYS TO USE THIS QUESTION

- A candid self-assessment tool for identifying where you're messing up or how you're most likely to mess up in the near future.

- A good question to ask to raise motivation levels on Friday mornings, especially when people seem to be overly concerned about their weekend plans.

- Helps people look at problems from the organizational perspective; gives everyone insight into the economic realities of downsizing, layoffs, etc.

A number of people gathered around the conference table had offered compelling reasons why they might lose their jobs. Just about every employee attributed the loss to economic misfortunes caused by competitor inroads or the need to invest in new technology. It was an interesting discussion in that it demonstrated how fearful everyone was about an economic downturn and the repercussions—clearly no one in the room felt that the organization would do everything it could to preserve their jobs.

Then a woman spoke up and said that if she were to be fired, she hoped it was because her poor performance merited it. She said she couldn't believe the organization would be so stupid as to fire a high-performing employee; that there would be choices involved, and they would choose to fire the mediocre ones. "If I'm going to get fired," she concluded, "I hope it's because I deserve that fate or at the very least because I called my boss an S.O.B."

You'll find a certain amount of defensiveness and denial accompanying this question. People aren't going to explore their feelings and ideas if you settle for answers like, "Oh, if I were to be fired, it probably would be because of a downsizing" or "I don't think it would be because of anything job-related."

Help make it personal. Get people to open up with the following questions:

- Even if you've never made a major blunder on the job, suggest the most likely one you might make in the future. If you made that blunder, would you deserve to be fired?

- Name someone who actually has been fired recently. Why was he or she fired? Do you feel the firing was justified? Might you be fired for a similar or related reason?

- When the organization fires someone, does it do so primarily for economic reasons? For political reasons? For personal reasons?

- Why would you fire someone? Under what conditions would you fire a coworker, your boss, or the CEO?

Which of these CONCEPTS— teamwork, learning organization, continuous improvement, leadership and quality— is the BIGGEST joke at your company

FOUR GREAT WAYS TO USE THIS QUESTION

- Gives junior and mid-level employees a chance to sound off about a prized management initiative that is laughed at by the rank and file.

- Offers management the opportunity to find out what the rank and file really think of their prized initiatives.

- Helps to measure the gap between theory and implementation; a starting point to figure out what might have gone wrong.

- A fun alternative to the typically deadly analytical approach companies use when talking about things like leadership and quality; gives a discussion a real-world flavor rather than the more academic tone people usually take.

WAR STORY

Perhaps the most alarming response to this question came from a team of junior people at a high-tech organization in the West. Before the meeting, we had told the manager responsible for this team—a veteran human resources executive—that we were going to ask this question. She didn't think we'd get a good response, explaining that the only initiative that the company had problems with was its quality one; she even showed us the results of an internal employee survey related to some of the terms in the question. Nonetheless, we asked it, and while some people named "quality" as the biggest joke, others named the four other terms, and one person even came up with a term not on the list (rightsizing), while another said, "All of the above." The resulting discussion alarmed the HR people sufficiently that they had us ask the question of other teams, and the responses were similar. All this prompted the organization to take a long, hard look at its initiatives and start the process of re-strategizing them.

USER'S MANUAL

This question usually results in polar opposite responses. Either people are willing to lambaste a particular initiative or they're too loyal to the company to criticize any of them. Expect critical and uncritical responses such as:

We keep getting charged with taking ownership of the current fad-of-the-day. But when we try to implement a program, like the team-building one, there's no support.

I cringe when a hot new management book catches on or they bring in a guru to talk to us. Now we're doing all these things to become a learning organization because of

Senge's book, but no one here really understands what a learning organization is let alone how to become one.

I wouldn't call any of those terms a joke here; I wouldn't feel comfortable singling any one out. I think we do a good job in all the areas you mentioned.

To help people think more deeply about this issue and discuss it productively, challenge their assumptions. For instance, we've found that when people call a particular term a joke, it's important to get them to be specific about their feelings:

Is it a joke because of how it's being implemented?

Is the concept a joke?

Is it a joke just to the person answering the question or to everyone in the department?

Can something be done to make it less of a joke?

Be aware that some people respond that a particular initiative is a joke because it requires them to change the way they work. The initiative may be viable, but it's their resistance to change that causes them to criticize it. Steer the discussion toward this resistance-to-change topic if you feel this is the case.

If, on the other hand, everyone is reluctant to criticize, make the question less threatening:

Of the terms mentioned, which one causes you the most headaches on a daily basis?

Whether you call it a headache or a joke, you want people to examine and discuss this question from an emotional standpoint rather than an intellectual one. That way, you'll learn things about initiatives that you'd never know if you simply asked, "What do you think of our leadership programs?"

40

What PROVERB captures the essence of your organization

TWO GREAT WAYS TO USE THIS QUESTION

- A good way to cut through complexity and get at the heart of an issue; provides a starting point for a discussion when people get sidetracked on tangential issues.

- Since everyone has a favorite proverb, this question usually does a nice job of catalyzing debate.

WAR STORY

A company had been to the brink of bankruptcy and barely avoided falling over the edge. This organization had once been a major player in its industry but a series of bad decisions had placed them far back in the pack. On top of all this, their main manufacturing plant had been partially destroyed by fire and the CEO hired to turn the company around had dropped dead of a heart attack three weeks after being hired. Amazingly, the company had managed to rebound from these disasters, and a slow, steady climb to profitability had resulted. An executive from the company didn't have to ponder what proverb answered the question for him: "Don't cry over spilled milk."

USER'S MANUAL

Expect these negative responses to this question:

I don't know any proverbs.
What does a proverb have to do with what our organization is all about?
Can't I just say what the essence of the company is and skip the proverb?

Having a list of proverbs ready will help you avoid negative answers and facilitate positive ones. Confronted with the list, people either will choose one that they think applies to the company or will be reminded of others. Here are some familiar proverbs:

- A stitch in time saves nine.
- Better safe than sorry.
- He who hesitates is lost.

- A fool and his money are soon parted.
- Don't count your chickens before they're hatched.
- Better to have loved and lost than never to have loved at all.
- Nothing ventured, nothing gained.

Use this exercise as another option: Instead of choosing a proverb, allow people to make one up. This is a lot of fun and people come up with everything from the truly wise to the truly wacky. A variation on this theme is to have people take a familiar proverb and twist it to fit the company. For instance: "Don't count your innovative products until R&D hatches them ..and manufacturing makes them."

No matter how you come up with proverbs, discussion should start with whether the proverbs reflect a positive or negative truth about the organization. If you're doing this exercise in a group, you're bound to get a mixture of good and bad as well as some ambiguous responses. Debates about the proverbs usually heat up when people start talking about why they think they capture a negative or positive truth about the company.

Additional questions to ask during the discussion are:

- Who would be most likely to agree with your chosen proverb: management or line workers?
- What proverb do you wish were true of your organization?
- What's the wisest thing about your company? What policy, procedure, or cultural aspect demonstrates an understanding of what employees or organizations need to grow and prosper?

41

How would GENE SISKEL and Roger Ebert review your department's performance

THREE GREAT WAYS TO USE THIS QUESTION

- As a vehicle for individuals to critique their own perfor- mance in more dramatic terms than usual; takes some of the sting out of the critique because it's done in fun.

- As a tool for teams to evaluate their performance in pro–con style (half the team is Ebert, half is Siskel).

- As a way for managers to evaluate organizational per- formance "from the balcony" rather than as participants in the drama.

WAR STORY

A sales executive asked this question at her weekly sales meeting. She divided the staff into two groups—Ebert and Siskel—and asked them to critique their sales meetings of the past year. Her only qualification was that the two groups must take opposing viewpoints. The Ebert group began by insisting the meetings were dull, the story lines were predictable ("people make excuses for not meeting quotas and brag when they exceed them"), and there wasn't enough action to hold anyone's interest. Thumbs down was their conclusion.

The Siskel group offered an enthusiastic thumbs-up review, saying that everyone fulfilled their roles beautifully, that speeches during the meetings were eloquent and inspirational, and there was great ensemble work.

As the debate went back and forth, everyone became aware of what was both positive and negative about the meetings. It wasn't that people previously had been unaware of these things. It was simply that the question forced people to think and talk about these issues rather than letting them lie dormant or be the subject of offhand comments around the coffee machine.

USER'S MANUAL

This question invites people to ham it up, and that's terrific. You want people to get into their roles as critics, since that's what's going to uncover the positive and negative aspects of performance.

We've found that this question is a nice supplement to drier performance evaluations; it's the essay test that accompanies the multiple-choice one. People enjoy the opportunity to dramatize their ideas about how well or poorly they or others performed.

Because people tend to get carried away in their "reviews"—especially when teams are divided into Siskel and Ebert—it helps to keep people's comments relatively brief. Our experience tells us that it also makes sense to stop reviews when they reach extremes to do a reality check. If, for instance, someone calls the department's performance "abysmal," ask the person to cite a specific incident to back up that criticism.

42

If YOUR company were a football team, what would be your STRONGEST and weakest positions?

THREE GREAT WAYS TO USE THIS QUESTION

- A great way to get people to analyze the company from a purely competitive perspective.

- A fun tension-breaker during strategic planning meetings.

- An alternative method to discuss the company's leadership (quarterback), competencies (skill positions such as running back, wide receiver), labor force (the offensive line), etc.

One of the best answers to this question that we've ever heard came from a cross-functional team assembled to analyze work flow policies. During the meeting, they'd been talking about their frustrations in trying to deal with an enormous workload and coordinate myriad activities. When we asked them the football question, they responded that their strength was quarterback, because their CEO was a visionary whose innovative ideas had helped the company grow by leaps and bounds. They added that their weakest position was also quarterback, because their visionary CEO was great at coming up with a game plan and awful at executing it; he was bored after he came up with terrific ideas and neglected to provide teams with the resources they needed to solve the problems that came with his brainstorms.

USER'S MANUAL

Some people may offer answers to this question that state the obvious and don't really take you anywhere. For instance:

- Our strongest position is quarterback because our CEO is a great leader, and we don't have a weak position.
- Our department is like the backfield of a football team; we always take the ball and score. All the other departments are like big, fat tackles or guards—they don't really serve much of a function except to clear the way for us.

To help yourself or others really think about this question, try the following exercise. We've listed each position on a football team, and your assignment is to name the player in your company who best fits that position; you can name more than one player per position. Then grade each player on an A+ to F scale, based on the position description (rather than your perception of his or her performance).

Position	Description	Names	Rating
Center	Always in the middle; primary protector of quarterback, who leads the play.		
Offensive linemen	Work closely with the center; team players; low profile; hard workers.		
Receivers	Highly skilled, very quick on feet, capable of spectacular plays. Enjoy the limelight, can be showboats.		
Fullback	Uses force rather than finesse to get job done; powerful, steady worker.		
Halfback	Looks for opportunistic openings, moves quickly, prefers running around instead of through obstacles.		
Quarterback	Team leader. Either likes to make plays singly or hand the ball off or pass with great precision.		

Position	Description	Names	Rating
Defensive linemen	Great at brushing aside obstacles to reach goals; fierce, dedicated, and able to play in pain.		
Linebackers	Versatile, able to stop, run, or pass; able to think on feet and change approach at a moment's notice.		
Defensive backs	Individualists, love to be out there alone testing themselves, willing to take chances to turn things around.		

As you review the grades for each person listed, ask the following questions:

- How can you better use those A- and B-graded positions to maximize their impact on the company?

- How can you upgrade the C- and D-graded positions to minimize the harm they do?

- Do the letter grades explain why certain decisions are made? Why you (your team, your department, your company) never achieve your goals? Why certain tasks are easier to perform than others?

Another way to spin off analysis from this question involves a different type of rating exercise. It's designed to help you view your organization as a competitive team, one that may be the Dallas Cowboys or the New York Jets of your industry. Rate your organization's capabilities on a 1 to 5 scale (1 being the lowest score) in the following areas:

Agility (flexibility, ability to change)   _____
Game plan (strategic planning)   _____
Speed (decision making and implementation)   _____
Level of talent (skills in key areas)   _____
Experience (veteran savvy)   _____
Attitude (enthusiasm, morale)   _____
Competitiveness (fierce or mild)   _____
Work ethic (willingness to go the extra mile)   _____

Total   _____

37-40 points   —Dominating franchise
32-36 points   —Always challenges leaders, never becomes
                      one
28-31 points   —Rebuilding year
24-27 points   —Doormat
23 points or below—Doesn't belong in the league

What would appear BIZARRE, shocking, or amazing to a MARTIAN visiting you at work

TWO GREAT WAYS TO USE THIS QUESTION

- Helps people practice thinking about what they do from an outside rather than inside perspective; reminds everyone how easy and dangerous it is to maintain an insular mind-set.

- Offers a fresh perspective on work; stimulates discussion of the meaning of work and why we do what we do.

WAR STORY

A sales team had gathered to talk about the problem they had distributing leads in a fair and equitable manner. During the meeting, which we were facilitating, a variation of this question came up. One person maintained that if an alien were to observe how they distributed leads, it might ask: "Why do Sue and George receive the most and the best leads, since neither one has the third eye that signifies royalty on our planet?"

The question defused the tension surrounding this issue and allowed for a discussion of the issue that didn't get bogged down in ad hominem arguments. (Whenever it verged on doing that, we brought our aliens back to ask another question.)

USER'S MANUAL

We receive many funny responses to this one, such as:

Why do people spend so much time sitting around oval tables eating doughnuts?
Why does that man in the corner office act like the ruler of Star 49?
Who is this downsizing fellow and why is everyone so afraid of him?

The best way to use the humor this question generates is as a way into sensitive subjects. The question of an observant alien can reveal a great deal about work behaviors. Encourage people to have their aliens ask acutely-observed questions. Have them focus on the five senses of the alien (and feel free to suggest a sixth and seventh sense if you want):

- What does the alien see, hear, feel, smell, and taste when he observes you at work?
- What shocks the alien?
- What pleases the alien?
- What is completely incomprehensible to the creature?
- What behavior might the alien misinterpret?

44

What would happen if your company instituted a one-year ban on meetings

TWO GREAT WAYS TO USE THIS QUESTION

- A lively discussion always results when people imagine a work world without meetings; it gets everyone thinking about the purpose of meetings.
- A good springboard for evaluating what types of meetings are useful and what types are wasteful.

WAR STORY

We'd like to depart from our usual war story format to share a personal experience that reveals the genesis of this question (and why we feel it's a good cage-rattler).

I (Dick) used to work for an ad agency that regularly met with a major unit of a client located a few blocks from our office. At least three times a week we'd meet to discuss strategy, brainstorm new advertising tactics, and drink a lot of coffee. It wasn't that the meetings were unproductive; some were very good. The majority, however, weren't really necessary. Or rather, much of what went on in them could have been handled on the phone or by letter. Still, we had fallen into a routine that was reassuring to both the agency and the client.

Then the client company relocated to Asia. They remained our client, but meetings and consumption of coffee declined precipitously. We could only meet two or three times a year, but these meetings were incredibly productive. Because we recognized that we had to plan and prepare for the meetings diligently, we put a lot of effort into doing so and arrived at the meetings prepared and energized.

In a sense, our "ban" on meetings helped us realize that: 1. we didn't need a lot of them to accomplish our goals, and 2. focusing energy, attention, and planning on a few meetings can greatly enhance their value.

USER'S MANUAL

When we ask this question of a group, they usually cheer. Most people hate meetings with a passion reserved for mosquitos and used-car salespeople. As a result, employees often respond that nothing bad would happen if meetings were banned for a year.

Challenge that assumption. It's not that meetings are worthless; it's that we have too many of them, they go on for too long, and they're not planned properly.

Here are some follow-up questions to lead a discussion in a productive direction:

- What was the best meeting you had in the past year? What was the worst?

- If your company or team went a year without meetings, how would you assign work, generate new ideas, get consensus on decisions, and assess progress toward goals?

- Who would be most resistant to banning meetings? Who would be most in favor of it?

45

What are the TOP TEN reasons YOUR people won't get the bonuses they deserve NEXT year**?**

FOUR GREAT WAYS TO USE THIS QUESTION:

- Gets the reasons on the table before management does so you'll steal some of their thunder.

- A tool to evaluate whether people really deserve bonuses.

- A way to counter unduly optimistic forecasts that have people counting their bonuses before they're hatched.

- Reminds managers that the best way to know a company is by the excuses it gives for not issuing bonuses.

As people answer this question, their responses form a pattern we'd like to share with you. While the responses are often different, the chronology is often the same. It will start you thinking about the false optimism that permeates corporate cultures at the beginning of the year. We call it: "Why bonuses are often like phases of the moon."

Full Moon: The bonus forecast at the beginning of the year usually starts with a full moon: "Things are really looking up; hit those easy performance goals and we'll be in hog heaven next summer."

Quarter Moon: In the second quarter management starts hedging their bets. They issue gentle reminders of everyone's fiscal responsibility, "particularly in these increasingly tight times."

Half Moon: At this phase the company has problems with the original forecast (particularly with the incentives).

Three Quarter Moon: By the fourth quarter everyone's reflecting on the sacrifices needed this year. The upside, of course, is that as a result of these sacrifices, "we're poised for a very lucrative future, starting the next fiscal year (or the next full moon)."

You can tell a lot about what's wrong with an organization from the excuses they give for a bonus-less year. The following exercise is only partially tongue-in-cheek. Try examining the ten common excuses and what they really mean. Then provide your company's version of a given excuse. Consider the thinking behind the excuse and what it says about your company.

1. *A softening economy created a dismal operating environment.*

Translation: *While our primary competitor's sales grew 20 percent.*

Your Version: _____

_____

2. *Our industry is experiencing a downturn.*

Translation: *The company once again missed reading the trends.*

Your Version: _____

_____

3. *We're sacrificing now to invest in the future.*

Translation: *A future use we may have sacrificed too much to see.*

Your Version: _____

_____

4. *The company had record sales, so we've had to commit to capacity growth.*

Translation: *We value growth more than we do rewarding great performance.*

Your Version: _____

_____

5. *Foreign exchange rates created an unfavorable balance.*

Translation: *Our foreign operations aren't doing so well.*

Your Version: _____

_____

6. *Customers in two major segments reduced orders.*

Translation: *They forecasted correctly; we didn't.*

Your Version: _____

_____

7. *The strike at the plant had a dramatic impact on results.*

Translation: *Put the blame there; nobody likes them anyway.*

Your Version: _____

_____

8. *Margins were squeezed by our distributors.*

Translation: *They've discovered how to run their business better.*

Your Version: _____

_____

9. *We're restructuring the incentive system to be more rewarding.*

Translation: *Only not this year.*

Your Version: _____

_____

10. *We've had to absorb unexpected write-offs.*

Translation: *The accountants will wordsmith this catch-all (and don't forget the 200-person management retreat to the private island in the Pacific).*

Your Version: _____

_____

46

What's your idea of a utopian workplace

THREE GREAT WAYS TO USE THIS QUESTION

- Allows employees to communicate their work dreams to management.

- Helps create a plan to improve the environment, policies, and other things that impact employee satisfaction.

- A positive way to have a discussion about problems in an organization; by talking about workplace utopia, people can couch their complaints in dreams of what they'd like rather than complaints about what they lack.

Have you ever heard the saying, "One man's heaven is another man's hell"? The union workers who addressed this question found the saying to be appropriate. One would talk about how the ideal job would have a ten-hour work week, and another would respond that he'd feel lazy and worthless if he only worked ten hours a week. Someone wished that her compensation would be equal to the CEO's, but then somebody else noted that if they were all being paid like kings, the company wouldn't survive. Interestingly, the utopian elements that the group agreed about tended to be small things: longer lunch breaks, more vacation time, an on-site day care center, an employee health club, less demanding supervisors, more flexible benefits and hours. They also agreed that their consensus version of utopia wasn't a total fantasy; that it was more a matter of eliminating some negative things in their workplace than creating a new workplace from scratch.

USER'S MANUAL

Utopia for some people consists of huge salaries, lots of vacation time, and short working hours. Try to move the discussion past utopian dreams to utopian realities. You can spend hours wishing you earned a higher salary, received all those unbelievable perks, or could open an office in Hawaii.

Concentrate on what's ideal but possible. Here are some suggestions for doing so:

- Create a list of wonderful innovations and policies at other organizations. They can include everything from working-at-home options to shared jobs. See which of these things the group believes fit the idea of utopia.

- What policy, person, or other aspect of the work environment would the group eliminate to move the company closer to utopia?

- What piece of utopia does the organization already have? Is there a perk or particular aspect of work life that's the envy of others outside the company?

How would the WORLD'S biggest cynic scorch Your ORGANIZATION

TWO GREAT WAYS TO USE THIS QUESTION

- Identifies the difference between the most hopeful reality and the most pessimistic perception; demonstrates the gap between the corporate ideal and the employee reality.

- Gives everyone a free shot at the company; allows the cynic in every employee to make the snide and cutting remarks he or she has always wanted to make.

WAR STORY

All the employee literature in Company ABC is filled with humanistic verbiage: "We care about our employees"; "a family atmosphere"; "we want to know what our people think." At a small, closed-door session with four randomly chosen employees of ABC, we found that one person didn't buy the propaganda.

William maintained that the company only cared about "top executives and minorities who might sue the company for discrimination. They care least about middle-aged white men who work in lower-level positions." William seemed to love his chance to play the cynic; he scorched management for its "extreme apathy toward its white male factory-floor workers."

The other three people in the room (two were women, one was black) disagreed with William about the specifics of his cynicism but agreed with his larger point. They all said that they felt the company didn't care about them, that it was all talk and no action.

Company ABC is currently interviewing and surveying other employees to determine if there is widespread agreement with the cynical comments of the four employees.

USER'S MANUAL

Cynicism is easy. That's why it makes a good departure point for discussion and debate. But it's also easy to get carried away with one's cynicism. We've seen people try to top each other with cynical comments just for entertainment value.

The main purpose of this question is to find the area where there's a big gap between what the company says and what employees perceive. That's why you want to check for consensus on a given cynic's point of view. If there's no consensus, keep asking for other cynical perspectives until you find one that the group agrees on.

You may also find that people get stuck in one area and can't take a broader perspective. If this happens, suggest the following things that companies often preach, and see if the group has any cynical comments about the practice:

- We pay our people as well as or better than any competitive organization in our industry.

- Our company always puts our values above results.

- We take a long-term outlook on things; the short term really doesn't matter.

- We still strongly believe in reengineering; we stopped the program only because we had other more immediate concerns and not because of criticism from the media.

- This company promotes employees based solely on performance; age, sex, race, friendships, and other factors are irrelevant.

Who would finally be
able to solve your most
stubborn WORK problem:
a master psychologist,
a venture capitalist,
or an enforcer from
the MOB

THREE GREAT WAYS TO USE THIS QUESTION

- Helps individuals and teams to discern their particular style of problem solving—and vent some frustration in the process.
- Gives people a chance to evaluate their problem-solving efforts from a fresh perspective.
- Helps people to define what they really need in terms of resources, support, and assistance to solve problems.

WAR STORY

A group of highly creative people in a consulting firm were initially divided when they attempted to answer this question. They had more than a passing familiarity with getting stuck—their clients had given them highly challenging assignments in the past year. Some of the group argued eloquently that a psychologist would help them deal with neurotic clients who didn't realize they were part of the problem. Others convincingly posited that a venture capitalist would provide the financing necessary to expand marketing budgets, open global offices, and fund other projects their clients couldn't afford. But the mob enforcer choice ultimately won the day. As one participant put it, "We get stuck because we're wimps."

The group agreed that they often became stymied because they didn't have the courage of their convictions. The group recalled a number of great ideas in the past year that never went anywhere because the client rejected them and no one stood up to defend the idea. Though the solution wasn't threatening the client with bodily harm, the group agreed that they'd be better off if they were more forceful in presenting what they felt were great ideas.

USER'S MANUAL

As the war story indicates, groups often clash over this question. The goal, however, isn't as much to choose the person who would best solve problems as it is to express ideas about possible causes and solutions.

If a group gets stuck arguing about which of the three people suggested is the right one, gently point out to them that they're "mirroring" the question by their behavior: Which one of the three would solve their problem of choosing one of the three?

Sometimes it helps to translate the three characters into the solutions they represent: psychologist (dealing effectively with irrational, stubborn, and otherwise difficult people); venture capitalist (funding for necessary resources, expansion, etc.); enforcer (taking a strong stand and convincing others of the rightness of a position).

If the discussion gets snagged on "how we always get stuck," share with the group the following stuck and unstuck behaviors:

Stuck people: Refuse to admit there might be a better way; become angry and blame others; view problems from individual rather than team perspectives.

Unstuck people: Keep open minds; assume there is an answer; give themselves a day or two of rest from the problem to gain insight; take collective responsibility for the problem.

49

You've just heard that all SALARIES, bonuses, and other compensation will now be based only on TEAM performance; how do you feel about this NEW POLICY

TWO GREAT WAYS TO USE THIS QUESTION

- Gives you a sense of how people are reacting to team-based structures; the compensation issue is just a wedge to get people to open up about their teams.

- Generates ideas from individuals about compensation, whether it should be tied to performance, and if it should be individual or team-based or a combination of the two.

Members of a recently formed work team at a manufacturing facility weren't enthusiastic about the prospect raised by this question. Only one person on the team was positive about a team-based compensation system. The others all felt that it would be unfair: that nine of them might do a great job but they'd be at the mercy of the one person who screwed up. Soon the group wasn't talking about compensation but was answering the unasked question: Why does everyone fear that someone will screw up? Because working on a team was a relatively new experience for most of them, they realized, no one completely trusted the other people. This, they all admitted, could be a problem down the road. The realization prompted them to talk about ways they could get to know each other better and ended with consensus about meeting outside of work once a month for drinks, dinner, and a chance to communicate with each other in a more informal way.

USER'S MANUAL

Don't be surprised if the conversation segues from compensation to team-related issues. It also shouldn't come as any surprise that American employees especially view themselves as individuals first and team players second, and thus favor individual compensation.

Rather than beating a group over the head with the benefits of team compensation, it's useful to encourage them to explain why they fear team-based compensation. Sometimes, as in the war story, they fear that others on the team will negatively affect their compensation. Others are opposed on philosophical grounds or because it's impractical (Does everyone on the team receive the same salary?).

If you find people are becoming involved in an endless circle of debate over individual versus team compensation—and no new ideas are being offered—try some of the following questions:

- Would you mind being rewarded based on team performance if you were on a dream team that you had performed well with in the past?
- Would you be willing to accept a hybrid compensation system where your bonus, if not your salary, was based on team performance?
- Why do you think your organization might prefer team-based compensation?
- What do you enjoy about working on a team as opposed to working on your own? What do you dislike?
- If you were to put a team together to go after an important new goal in your area, who would you put on the team and how would you motivate them?

50

What HORRENDOUS blunder
did you (or others)
make in the past year?
What did you LEARN
from it

FOUR GREAT WAYS TO USE THIS QUESTION

- Teaches a group that mistakes and failures can be positive experiences; for use by a company that wants to encourage risk-taking and is willing to accept a certain amount of failure in the process.

- Reduces the anxiety about making mistakes that sometimes exists in teams; helps people learn to laugh at their mistakes and realize that they aren't the end of the world.

- A standard question for any company that aspires to the status of "learning organization."

- Identifies patterns in mistake-making; examines the underlying reasons behind common mistakes so people can take steps to prevent them.

WAR STORY

Board members of a not-for-profit organization quickly agreed that their most horrendous mistake was hiring an executive director who was utterly incompetent when it came to raising funds. As good as she was as a manager, this executive director couldn't raise a penny at a billionaire's ball, so they had canned her. The board members strongly disagreed that any learning had taken place. The mistake had plunged the organization into troubled financial waters that they had only recently climbed out of because each board member had spent a great deal of time and effort appealing for funds from influential people and companies.

"It was an out-and-out catastrophe," they maintained.

"But didn't you learn that the board has the ability to raise a great deal of money quickly if necessary?"

"Yes," they grudgingly admitted.

"Didn't you learn that it was wise to separate the association's managerial role from the fund-raising role by hiring two different people?"

"Yes, that was true."

"And didn't you learn that the board should monitor fund-raising efforts more closely and more frequently so that the situation doesn't recur?"

"Okay," they admitted, "some learning took place."

USER'S MANUAL

The key in using this question is to move people past the "woe is me" stage. As the war story indicates, a few questions can reveal the learning that emerged from the horrendous mistake. To ask those questions, you need to get people to tell you the consequences of the mistake.

This is a question that works especially well with younger employees; older ones often have learned that success can be built on failure.

Also, be sure to ask this question to get a group thinking proactively:

- What can you do to increase the odds that you won't make the same horrendous blunder again?

51

You've just received $10 MILLION to help the company grow and prosper; how would you SPEND it?

FOUR GREAT WAYS TO USE THIS QUESTION

- Stimulates thinking about budgeting from a high-ground perspective.

- A great way to get people who are always complaining about a lack of resources to articulate what resources they really need and how they would use them.

- Enables people to get a sense of the relationship between money and adding value.

- Let's money-starved employees loose in a financial candy store of the mind; put in a less metaphorical way, it allows people the creative freedom to think of tactics and strategies without considering the usual budgetary constraints.

Here's a note we received from a veteran manager in response to this question: "I'd take the money and set up a fund that would give individual employees, teams, and departments 'grants' for projects they wanted to pursue but couldn't afford to given their budgets. It would be similar to funds set up by foundations to help innovators and artists pursue worthwhile projects. What it would mean is that whenever an employee or a team had something that was shot down when they went through normal channels (a common occurrence in our organization) they could take the alternative route of applying for a grant. If they received it—a committee would be set up to determine who should get these grants—they would automatically receive permission from management to pursue their project under guidelines set up by the committee. The incentive for applying for these grants would be bonuses and other compensation if a project had a positive outcome."

Be prepared for responses that range from the silly to the sublime:

Silly: I'd give myself one heck of a raise; of course I'd also work harder, which would allow the company to grow and prosper.

Sublime: I'd use all of it on people—some of it would go to pay our best people what they deserve so they wouldn't leave; some of it would go to hire people with the expertise we lack; and some of it would be put into a leadership incentive pool to reward the relatively few people who take risks and have a vision for the organization.

In between the silly and sublime there are all sorts of responses:

- I'd put it in a special training fund for ongoing programs.
- I'd invest it in new product development and building a state-of-the-art research facility.
- I'd divide the company into business units and institute gain-sharing.

Encourage people to be imaginative rather than practical with their suggestions. With this question, it pays to be weird, wild, provocative, and innovative. The follow-up question to use, of course, is:

- Is there anything in your highly imaginative ideas that we can actually use to help the company grow and prosper?

Surprisingly, usable ideas are often revealed as the group strips away the layers of wishing and fantasy.

52

What are the TOP FIVE
excuses people give
for MISSING a deadline

FOUR GREAT WAYS TO USE THIS QUESTION

- Helps you and others start taking deadlines seriously.
- A way to inform everyone at the start of a project or during a launch meeting which five deadline-related excuses will not be acceptable.
- Pinpoints what's behind the excuses people commonly offer.
- A tool for time management.

At a meeting of a group of engineers employed by a well-known manufacturer, the most common excuse offered was: "The deadline was unreasonable." At first, they complained about all the unreasonable deadlines they received and claimed that this wasn't an excuse, it was a justified complaint. After they had this excuse out of their systems, we nudged them backwards, asking them why they didn't complain about the deadline when they originally heard what it would be. "Because our culture is one of tight deadlines," said one. "It wouldn't be politic to complain up front," said another. Yet it was clear that missed deadlines made managers furious, and that they messed up production schedules and cost the company a good deal of money. When it came down to it, the group agreed that they would receive less flak if they complained about the deadline sooner rather than later. The rest of the meeting was spent discussing ways of broaching this sore subject with management.

USER'S MANUAL

Though there are a million excuses for missing deadlines, they all fall into five general categories. You might want to start a discussion by listing the categories and an example of a common excuse in each. Add the one that you hear the most (or use the most yourself) in each category.

Time:

I'm not going to turn this in until it's right, no matter how long it takes.

It just isn't physically possible to do it within the time frame.

Other Priorities:

Jane needed my help, and her project was an emergency so I thought that was more important.

The customer asked me to do this for him, and I assumed customers come first.

Emotional:

..and it turned out I had my kids for the weekend.

I'm just so overworked and stressed out, I just blocked this assignment out, I feel awful …

Strange but probably true:

So there was my towed car in the compound with all my materials for the project.

Maybe it was a power surge, but the computer lost a week's work.

Pure fabrications:

My grandmother died.
You never told me when it was due.
No one's ever held me to a deadline before.

Now have everyone think about the category for each excuse you listed with the following in mind: "Time" excuses can be legitimate—think about whether the deadline was fair. "Other priorities" can involve politics or genuine misunderstandings; is this the case here or is it an invented priority? "Emotional" excuses can be genuine calls for help or they can be the most blatant form of manipulation. "Strange but probably true" excuses often reflect bad luck. "Pure fabrications" are the sign of someone who is lazy, uncaring, or thinks you're a gullible moron.

Here's another way to look at it and talk about it: When you catch someone making a deadline excuse, ask:

a. Why is the excuse usually made? b. Is there some justi-
fication for the excuse? c. Is the person who made the excuse completely at fault, partially at fault, or a victim of cir-
cumstance? d. What will be the result of the excuse—what
harm will be done by the missed deadline?

How might you SABOTAGE a new process, policy, or PROCEDURE? What could motivate YOU

THREE GREAT WAYS TO USE THIS QUESTION

- Determines the level of change resistance in a group or the organization; measures how much people hate a new system by how much they want to sabotage it.

- Warns the company about how employees might sabotage a hated new process, policy, or procedure; tells them which ones employees despise more than life itself.

- A good tool to analyze whether an existing process, policy, or procedure should be changed; this question serves as a straw poll of employees.

An organization wanted to get a sense of how employees would feel if they installed new software, so they gathered a group of employees together and asked them this question. Management had anticipated some resistance. What they hadn't anticipated was the glee and inventiveness the employees brought to the question. The employees came up with one ingenious form of sabotage after another: Pretending they didn't understand how to use the new software and intentionally screwing up the way they entered data was one of them. It was clear from the employees' reaction that the company would be asking for trouble if they brought in new software without first educating employees about how it would work and how it would help make their jobs easier.

When you ask this question, you may receive the following question in response:

Describe the process, policy, or procedure.

It's good to have one handy to describe. You don't want to stack the deck too much by trashing a favorite employee policy; tell the group that you're going to reduce lunch breaks by 15 minutes and you'll receive a lot of sabotage suggestions.

Choose something that seems to have positive and negative consequences—a new process that will reduce the amount of time it takes employees to do a job but that will require an initial investment of three weekends of time for training in the new process.

When there are a lot of ingenious sabotage ideas and people are very enthusiastic about them, it's a good sign that the process, policy, or procedure is flawed.

54

Why and when does the organization make you feel that the information you need is top SECRET and you're a poor security risk**?**

THREE GREAT WAYS TO USE THIS QUESTION

- As a grassroots evaluation of the information flow in your organization; to determine if people are really getting the information they need when they need it.

- Gauges a company's empowerment efforts; indicates if people have been given decision-making responsibility without the necessary information.

- Inspires creative thinking about information; helps open people's eyes to the power of knowledge and the need to make it accessible quickly.

WAR STORY

Management at a Fortune 500 company were concerned that their effort to drive the decision-making process downward wasn't working. Despite their attempts to get people closest to the action to make decisions, there was still reluctance to do so. And when employees did make decisions, they made them slowly and often showed errors in judgement.

We held a number of meetings with different teams in an attempt to get to the root of the problem. We asked a number of our questions, and none of them yielded anything significant until we asked this one. All of a sudden, everyone was talking at once. Everybody had a story to tell about how they were refused access to data because it was "financial" or "strategic"; how the MIS system automatically shut people below management level out of certain files.

After much discussion, it was clear that people felt they were shut out of the data-gathering rather than the decision-making process. The company's fear that people didn't understand the decisions they were being called upon to make was groundless. The solution was a redesign of the company's information systems and the declassification of a great deal of material.

USER'S MANUAL

In some companies, information access is a touchy subject. Some organizations really believe that loose lips sink ships, that industrial espionage is rampant, and that the media are just waiting to get their hands on some combustible memo. We exaggerate. Still, some companies are a bit paranoid. If your company is, you may get "muted" responses to this question, such as:

Oh, it's not so bad as all that. Still, I guess there are times I wish I could get my hands on data more quickly.

Probing these responses is a good idea. It may be that the problem isn't that bad. Or it may be that people are nervous about admitting that management operates like the CIA. To find out, ask:

- What information would be really dangerous in the hands of competitors, the media, or other outside groups? Why? How much chance is there of that happening? Has it happened in the past?
- How frequently are you denied access to information? What are the most common types of information that you can't get your hands on?
- Who is stopping you from getting information? Is it orders from on high? Is it your direct superior? Is it difficult to determine who is stopping you?

55

What's your company's dirty LITTLE secret?

FIVE GREAT WAYS TO USE THIS QUESTION

- Helps people explore aspects of the organization that usually aren't discussed in public; provides a way to start talking about the unspoken policies and attitudes that shape the culture.

- A good forum for airing grievances; gives people an opening for discussing what bugs them about how the company operates.

- Helps identify a specific event or incident from the company's past that management may think has been forgotten but still impacts people (like a lawsuit, article in the newspaper, etc.).

- A forum for talking about "sensitive" issues like sexual harassment, diversity, and so on.

- Helps identify false rumors and enables the company to address them before they do any more damage.

The public relations department of a large manufacturer was meeting to discuss internal tactics such as the company newsletter when the head of the department asked this question. He asked it because of a negative employee survey; it was the first one with negative responses about management and leadership that he could remember. Perhaps there was something going on that he was unaware of. In response to the question, a number of people pointed to the rumor that the company had used a batch of inferior material for one of their product lines in order to save money, and that everyone involved in the process had been threatened with termination if they said one word about it.

The p.r. head later brought this rumor to the attention of management. They conducted an investigation, hiring an outside firm to assess if the rumor were true. When it was proved false, the company made the security firm's report available to everyone in the organization.

Sometimes people are very forthcoming with rumors and reports of everything from financial shenanigans to the CEO's odd sexual proclivities. In these instances, the discussion will probably take off as people debate whether these secrets are true or false.

In certain instances, however, the question may be met with silence. Either people don't believe the organization has any dirty little secrets or they don't know what they are.

It doesn't matter. The use of this question doesn't depend on a company having a sordid past or something it's trying to hide. The idea here is to get people thinking about what *might* be a secret, what could feasibly cause a problem if kept hidden. It enables a group to explore a company's sensitive subjects. The following exercise facilitates that exploration.

Ask a group to create a list of generic dirty little secrets or use the following list:

Secret meetings

Kickbacks

A suppressed survey or report

Sexual discrimination

Age discrimination

Racial discrimination

Questionable ethics

Doctored expense reports

Missing documentation

Nepotism

Favoritism

Rigged deals

Using this list, people should identify the secret that they think the company would most likely be trying to hide and then fabricate a scenario using real people employed by or involved with the company. The key to the discussion is in examining why a given scenario is possible.

If you could make a decision right now that would EITHER save the company $10,000 or cost them an equal amount, could you make it WITHOUT getting ANYONE'S approval **?**

FOUR GREAT WAYS TO USE THIS QUESTION

- Determines how people feel about empowerment; are they empowered to make meaningful decisions or meaningless ones?

- Gives employees a chance to clarify their decision-making responsibilities; are they empowered to make financial decisions versus nonfinancial ones?

- Produces challenging ideas about what empowerment policy should consist of; defines the parameters of decision making that seem fair and appropriate.

- Measures the comfort level of decision makers and whether they have sufficient information to make decisions with financial consequences.

WAR STORY

A group of young managers at a Fortune 100 company agreed that they were empowered to make decisions without approval involving the dollar amount specified in the question. In fact, three of the managers specified decisions they'd made in the last month that involved dollar amounts in excess of $100,000. They said further that management was very committed to its empowerment program and didn't second-guess the decisions made.

"Of course," one of the managers added in a lowered voice, "I really don't think I was qualified to make the decision."

What do you mean, we asked?

"I didn't have enough experience, I guess, though that's not really it. I authorized an additional $125,000 for promotional purposes for a product I handle. I thought it was the right thing to do, but I really wasn't sure if it was appropriate since I'd never authorized anything like that before. It would have made more sense if I could have talked to someone in the company about whether the extra money would really do much more to promote the product. It would have been good if I had to get advice from a senior person before deciding, if not actual approval."

Others in the room agreed that they sometimes felt they were on shaky ground when they made decisions, that they lacked the information that would make them more comfortable with their decisions. As a result of this meeting, the managers in the room decided that they would attempt to modify the company's empowerment policy so there was a "fail-safe" system of approval in place.

The way you lead this discussion depends on whether someone says yes or no in response to this question. If they say yes, ask:

- Do you feel confident in your ability to make the right decision?
- Do you wish you had a senior person to consult with about it?
- Have you ever been chastised for making the wrong decision?
- What would make it easier for you to make the right decision?

If they say no, ask:

- Is there a discrepancy between what the company's empowerment policy is and what you're entitled to decide?
- Do you feel that seeking approval is demeaning or hamstrings your decision-making ability?
- Who insists that you seek approval? Is it something you do automatically or is there a senior person who insists you get it?

We've found that a fertile area of exploration related to this question involves information. Time and again (and as the war story illustrates), people are empowered to make important financial decisions but lack the right information at the right time. You might want to steer the discussion toward this issue and determine whether people are receiving the information they need; you might also ask for suggestions about better ways to obtain the needed data.

57

If you could snap your FINGERS and turn your boss into a member of the opposite sex (or ANOTHER race, or change his or her age by 30 YEARS), what workplace issues might he or she BECOME more sensitive to **?**

FOUR GREAT WAYS TO USE THIS QUESTION

- Stimulates lively discussions about sexism, racism, and ageism.

- Helps people develop an appreciation for diversity.

- A good way to talk about potentially sensitive subjects using a distancing, humorous device.

- Enables bosses to glimpse ways they might improve as bosses that they would never have glimpsed before; gets male supervisors in touch with their feminine sides, allows white employees to develop sensitivity to minority issues.

WAR STORY

At a small, family-owned business, a group of factory employees invited the CEO to attend the meeting in which they responded to this question. The CEO was in his seventies and had run the business the same way for years. Though his employees liked him and thought him kind and generous, they felt many of his policies were hopelessly old-fashioned—he insisted on a rigid dress code, he forbade people to play any music on their radios except "classical" music, and he referred to women employees as "girls" and called them "honey."

In responding to the question, the group turned him into a young, black woman. The result was like a skit in which everyone took turns "imitating" this transformed CEO and issuing very new policies (the radio policy was that only hip-hop music, blues, and jazz could be played). The CEO was doubled over laughing at what everyone said, and he agreed to loosen up some of his long-standing rules for a test period; if it didn't negatively affect work performance, he'd make the changes permanent.

USER'S MANUAL

Be careful that responses to this question don't become insulting. Insensitive people can make sexist, racist, and ageist statements as they transform the boss. Caution people about being aware of other people's feelings before they metamorphose managers.

While the people in our war story invited the boss to the session, this isn't always a good idea. People need the freedom to be a bit outrageous, and they may not always feel they have that freedom if the boss is in the room.

New perspectives emerge when people really think about this question rather than offer funny, facile responses. How would things be different if a boss was a woman rather than a man? How would she treat people who made mistakes? How would she handle confrontations?

58

What INCREDIBLE invention would make your job much easier and you MUCH MORE productive

TWO GREAT WAYS TO USE THIS QUESTION

- Allows people to think about personal productivity from a purely mechanical perspective; talking about inventions instead of the usual productivity issues frees employees to explore the concept in new ways.

- Based on the "inventions" created, this question spawns ideas that can be translated into real productivity tools.

WAR STORY

George came up with a wonderful invention in response to our question. George is an advertising agency account executive who complained about how much time he spends on the phone and how little "thinking" time he has to plan marketing strategies and tactics for his clients. Every day, he said, he fields 30 or 40 phone calls from people asking questions that require some type of answer. While answering the questions doesn't take long, George feels obligated to talk to each person for a bit before hanging up. To save himself time, George invented a computer/phone device that is programmed to answer 100 of the most common questions asked; the computer phone would be programmed so that it would answer as George would depending on the information fed into it.

Though George's invention was pure fantasy, the idea behind it made sense. What came through loud and clear was that George needed an assistant, and his agency agreed that he was handling enough business to justify it. People at his level usually didn't have assistants, but this question communicated that an exception should be made in George's case.

USER'S MANUAL

Encourage people to be truly inventive. The value of this question is in stretching people's minds, in getting them to push beyond the stock productivity answers. Some people are going to suggest variations on inventions that already exist: a faster computer, more sophisticated software, a better-equipped company plane.

You want responses that are truly original:

- A market telescope that can spot markets just as they're emerging.
- A brain implant that culls creative ideas from dreams while people sleep.
- A virtual reality manufacturing machine that produces prototype products simply by hearing a description of what traits that product should have.

To spark these inventive ideas, loosen people up. Ask them to come up with equally inventive names for their inventions. Find out the specific benefits of their inventions in a work situation. Tell them to "make up" an explanation of how the invention functions.

All this will lead to a mind-boggling spectrum of ideas about increasing personal productivity.

59

What unwritten rules at work make it difficult to get things done quickly, efficiently, or profitably **?**

THREE GREAT WAYS TO USE THIS QUESTION

- Helps surface organizational norms that are so much a part of the culture that no one even thinks to question whether they're good norms.

- A good tool to solicit employee ideas about reducing cycle time, improving processes, and helping people to meet deadlines and add value.

- For discussions designed to allow people to air gripes, complaints, and general dissatisfaction with company policies.

During a meeting of managers at a highly paternalistic, family-owned business, this question was asked. After some hesitation, one of the managers said, "Maybe this is just me, but I always felt that if you fired someone who had more than five years tenure, you were risking your own career here." Immediately another manager concurred, mentioning that he had talked with a senior vice president about getting rid of someone he felt was a clearly incompetent employee, only to be told, "I think she deserves a second chance." The majority of the managers in the room agreed that they felt pressure to keep long-term employees, regardless of their negative job performance. The managers at the meeting decided to discuss this issue with the CEO. Rather than be defensive or deny that this situation existed, the CEO seemed honestly surprised. He admitted that when his father had run the company, no long-term employee was ever fired. When he took over, he recognized the paternalistic strain in the culture but didn't realize its impact on decision making. While the company couldn't eliminate the paternalistic culture overnight (nor, truth be told, did the CEO or other executives really want to eliminate it), they did address issues such as five-year tenure and made sure that performance rather than seniority was the deciding factor in such cases.

USER'S MANUAL

Here are some common responses to watch for that prevent this question from being used productively:

- What do you mean by "unwritten rules"?
- I don't think we have any.

- It's the written policies and procedures that cause me headaches.

If people don't understand what you mean by unwritten rules, define them as falling into one of the following three categories:

1. **Prohibitions.** These are things that everyone knows it's forbidden to do. Perhaps one unwritten rule is that you can't leave promptly at 5 p.m. every day (the culture says that people must work more hours than competitors—even if there's nothing to do).

2. **Procedures.** Work must be done in a certain way. For instance: Reports must be written in a way that incorporates certain favored business buzzwords and emphasizes the positive over the negative.

3. **Myths.** These often take the form of false truisms: "That idea has been presented and rejected for years."

If people claim the company doesn't have unwritten rules, cite the most common one of all:

Not invented here, not allowed here.

This means that if we didn't invent it here, we're not going to make it, sell it, or support it. Rather than purchase a superior technology, a company continues to rely on its inferior system. Even if this unwritten rule doesn't apply to a company, it's one that people recognize as applying to other organizations and usually prompts them to come up with one of their own.

If people persist in focusing on written rules, rephrase the original question as follows:

- Do you feel that anyone at your organization has been fired or promoted unfairly? Why?

Hiring and firing decisions often are influenced by unwritten rules, and this usually gets people thinking and talking about this subject.

60

Using your BEST IMITATION of Daffy Duck, Bart Simpson, or Beavis and BUTTHEAD, describe communication within your organization (or team, or department, or between you and your boss)

?

TWO GREAT WAYS TO USE THIS QUESTION

- Produces an animated discussion about communication that allows people to explore this usually sensitive topic in zany, unpredictable, and irreverent ways.

- Helps people talk about others who don't communicate well without feeling threatened; humor often takes the sting out of being told that you don't communicate well or telling someone else the same thing.

WAR STORY

A group of very somber accountants got together and started discussing communication issues in the voices of Porky Pig, Donald Duck, Homer Simpson, Mickey Mouse, and Elmer Fudd. Surprisingly, they were good mimics, and they were talking about serious issues in exceedingly unserious ways; the contrast made them and us crack up every few minutes. Afterward, they all noted that this approach made it much easier to air grievances about people "talking down" to junior members of the group and not sharing information with others. Or, as Porky put it: "Jim, if you d-d-don't tell me the next time when y-y-you're meeting with our client, I'm c-c-coming to your office with a baseball bat and you'll be the one saying, Th-th-th-that's all, folks."

USER'S MANUAL

Here are two problems you might encounter with this question: First, not everyone remembers or likes cartoon characters and some people are terrible at imitations. As a result, it may be that no one has anything to say in response to the question. Second, if you have a lot of goofy people in the group, the discussion can degenerate into silliness.

If the former happens:

- Name a bunch of cartoon characters and give people brief descriptions of each one. You might even want to bring a videotape of some cartoons to the meeting and play them before asking the question.

If the latter happens:

- Ask everyone to return to their un-cartoon-like selves and evaluate what a given cartoon character has said about a communication problem.

    Great discussions around this question often begin with great humor and inventiveness, but then settle down to a serious discussion of communication issues.

61

Do you EVER feel that if you're given one more piece of DATA, you might explode❓

THREE GREAT WAYS TO USE THIS QUESTION

- A way to bring all the talk about the information revolution down to real work terms; gives people a chance to talk about all the data flying across their desks and what they make of it.

- Helps MIS people understand the frustrations of ordinary people who can't process data as quickly or in as organized a fashion as a computer.

- A good starting point for a discussion on how to disseminate, sort, and use data.

After using this question with a group of employees who were extremely vocal in their complaints about "data overload," a senior manager who had been observing the session took us back to his office. It was a spacious corner office, which was a good thing. In one corner, there were stacks and stacks of bound reports with attractive, glossy covers.

"I know everyone in my group thinks they have too much information to deal with," he said. Then he pointed to the stacks of reports and said, "Those are all the reports we commissioned from consulting and research firms in the past two years. There's a lot of great information there. Too much great information. One firm's data seems to contradict another's. Another consulting firm's conclusion suggests we need to do even more research about a market. I know that feeling of an impending explosion."

As a result of his and the group's reaction to the question, they resolved to strategize a better way to make their database more usable and user-friendly.

USER'S MANUAL

We've found that when we ask this question, people respond that information is "suffocating," "overwhelming," and "confusing." We encourage people to be specific after they've expressed their anger and angst. What type of information are they drowning in? To help them get specific, we suggest the following categories:

- memos, e-mails, and voice mails
- reports (internal or external)
- articles

- books
- manuals
- videotapes
- multimedia (info from CD-ROMs, databases, etc.)

Next, we ask them who's giving them this information. Is a superior insisting they read it? Is there value in the information? What information could they easily do without? What information is critical? Is there a particular time of year when information overload is worse than others?

We've also found that people appreciate "sorting" ideas near the end of the discussion. Because the information revolution isn't going to go away, it helps to have some organizational or prioritizing system to deal with the data. Here are some tools along those lines:

- Sort information into three tiers: Tier One—Timely; Tier Two—Time will tell; Tier Three—Time will take care of. The last two piles don't require action and therefore can safely accumulate information without putting pressure on people to do anything about it.

- Sort information based on "asked for" versus "unsolicited." This will tell people if the problem is that they're asking for too much data or that they're on too many other individuals' junk mail lists.

62

CONGRATULATIONS! You've been offered a promotion. However, the new position requires spending the next two years in BULGARIA and the following two years in Zimbabwe. Would you accept it?

THREE GREAT WAYS TO USE THIS QUESTION

- Opens a discussion on company loyalty and commitment.

- Good way for an individual to identify feelings about working for a global organization.

- If an organization actually is opening an office in Bulgaria, Zimbabwe, or some other faraway place, this question helps you know who to send!

WAR STORY

A team had been formed at a large organization to help strategize how to help its people make the adjustment to working in the company's foreign offices. A significant percentage of the company's employees had difficulty making the adjustment, and some had quit or threatened to quit unless they were transferred back to the United States. While the company didn't have offices in Zimbabwe or Bulgaria, they did have a number of offices in third world countries. The team hadn't made much progress until this question was posed. Suddenly, the issue was personal and conflicted. Everyone agreed that a promotion would be a good inducement to move to a less-than-desirable spot. But there was a lot of debate around the issue of what people would be willing to sacrifice to get that promotion. One of the big issues that everyone agreed they wouldn't sacrifice was quality of life for their family—meeting the educational needs of their children abroad and jobs for spouses who worked were key considerations. As a result of this meeting, the team determined that the organization should assist relocating families in finding good schools and funding private education as well as actively helping spouses to find jobs.

USER'S MANUAL

You'll get the most out of this question if you substitute names of countries or specific locales that people in your organization dread going to. In addition, people may ask you to define exactly what a promotion would entail. We've found that the best way to do this is to suggest a promotion that's enticing but not overwhelmingly wonderful. You really want people to be torn between a good promotion and an undesirable country; if the promotion is a once-in-a-lifetime opportunity, everyone will say that they'd take it.

If you can't get any closure on this question—if everyone is waffling and saying things like, "Well, I might take it if ..."—try the following:

- Suggest some positive aspects of the country in question.
- Add that the company will provide certain incentives (salary or bonus, opportunity for advancement, travel allowance to make frequent trips back to the states, etc.).
- Suggest some negative aspects of the country in question.
- Add that this assignment is a privilege and that people shouldn't require extra incentives to recognize that it's a great opportunity.

Remember, the point of this question is to help people explore their feelings about working in other countries before they work there. It's a chance to see who is eager to do so, what the common objections and fears are, and so on. Try making the foreign posting more positive or more negative—whichever one you believe will foster expression of people's real feelings.

63

If you worked in a BIG glass fishbowl, what might you do DIFFERENTLY

FOUR GREAT WAYS TO USE THIS QUESTION

- Encourages people to scrutinize their work behaviors from the perspective of outsiders (there's nothing like being in a "fishbowl" to make you aware of bad or inappropriate work habits).

- Focuses attention on both negative and positive behaviors (what you want to hide, what you want to display proudly).

- Lets people consider what it would be like if while they worked they could observe bosses, customers, and suppliers, and what they might do differently.

- This is a neat way of opening a discussion about supervisory issues; do people feel that big brother is watching or that big brother doesn't care?

WAR STORY

A department had been reorganized into process-oriented teams and had been given increased decision-making power. One of the teams had been complaining that the team structure wasn't delivering the results everyone expected and no one could quite put a finger on the problem. When we asked the team the fishbowl question, though, it became clear what the problem was. Team member after team member said words to this effect: "If we were working in a fishbowl, we'd wave signs with the word, 'help' on them, and then at least management might pay more attention to our requests for better direction at the times when we need direction."

USER'S MANUAL

Here's what people say they'd do differently if they worked in a fishbowl:

- I'd work a lot harder if I knew I was being watched all the time.
- I'd quit because I hate being watched while I work.
- I'd ask for a big raise because my boss would know how much I really contribute.
- I wouldn't talk to my friends on the phone so much.

A lot of people focus on their negative behaviors, which is a natural response to this question. But if you want to broaden the responses, ask people to start thinking about the fishbowl as a work metaphor. It opens up discussion topics such as:

- The rights of workers to privacy.
- The concept of working behind closed doors individually versus working in an open area with team members.
- The ability of people to observe bosses (or customers or suppliers) and how *they* might react if they knew they were always being watched.

If people get stuck on negative behavior answers to this question, try varying the question as follows:

- If your team were working in a fishbowl in the CEO's office, what might you want him to observe you doing?

   Or:

- Who would attract the most positive attention on your team (or in your department) if you were all working in a fishbowl?

What BARNYARD animal would you choose as your TEAM or CORPORATE symbol

THREE GREAT WAYS TO USE THIS QUESTION

- Reduces all the complex ideas and feelings about an employer or other group to one powerful image; puts into a "picture" what often is difficult to put into words.

- It's fun to choose a mascot; the process of choosing a creature to represent the group yields fresh insights about the group's strengths and weaknesses.

- Facilitates discussion among marketing people about corporate identity advertising and other image-making issues.

WAR STORY

A team was divided by a version of this question: What type of creature (animal, insect, or fish) would you choose as your team or corporate symbol? Half of them insisted that a mule would best represent them since a lot of team members were stubborn and arrived at consensus slowly; they also said the team embodied the positive traits of a mule such as surefootedness, willingness to carry the load, and the ability to deliver a fierce kick. The other half of the team, however, opted for a dolphin because of its "cleverness and playfulness," maintaining that the team had a history of coming up with very inventive solutions to tough problems while maintaining a great sense of humor in the process.

The discussion illuminated the almost paradoxical qualities of the team; it gave everyone a sense of their strengths and weaknesses; and it fostered an understanding of the team's synergy and how they arrived at consensus. After spending a lot of time debating the subject, the team agreed that their symbol should be a hybrid creature called a Mulephin.

USER'S MANUAL

We've found that this question can produce a zoo-like diversity of creatures; everyone has his or her own favorite. That's okay, but make sure that people defend their choices and that their defense makes sense. Some people choose a creature for silly reasons; one person in a group we facilitated insisted that the corporate symbol should be a dragon because the CEO was a "fire-breathing monster." On the other hand, we recall an employee of a company that had just undergone a dramatic and successful transformation suggesting that the symbol should be a "butterfly emerging from a cocoon."

The latter symbol makes sense, and it's helpful to try to make a connection between the symbol and substantive business issues. Here are some follow-up questions that may help establish that connection during a discussion:

- If your chosen creature were imprinted on your building, on your stationery, and in all your advertising, would you feel comfortable with it?

- Think of the opposite of the creature you've picked; is it a symbol of everything your company or team is not?

- Does your creature embody both the strengths and weaknesses of your group, or is it symbolic only of the former or the latter?

- If you could combine two or three creatures in order to find an appropriate symbol, which ones would you combine?

65

Does the boss EVER punish people who tell her what she DOESN'T want to HEAR

FOUR GREAT WAYS TO USE THIS QUESTION

- A good managerial device to determine the issues that feel threatening to subordinates and suppliers; helps ferret out the areas where people may hide important information from you.

- A provocative opening for managerial meetings; gets executives nervous (some will feel strongly that their people aren't afraid of telling them any bad news; others will feel the opposite).

- A way to determine whether the organization is operating with one eye closed; whether the culture encourages or discourages the immediate communication of all news, whether good or bad.

- This question can be flipped around and used with non-managerial people: "Would you tell anyone bad news if ..?" Allows teams to bring into the open the existence of managers or policies that prevent open communication from flourishing.

WAR STORY

One of the more dramatic illustrations of this question took place a short time ago during an executive staff retreat. There were ten vice presidents of a rapidly-growing electronics company at the retreat, and the question was flipped around ("Would you tell bad news to someone if ..."). It provoked nothing more than embarrassed coughs and silence at first. Finally, one of the vice presidents suggested that their CEO was usually receptive to bad news, but when it came to his pet project, his attitude changed. The company had been working on a new executive desktop work unit that had great promise; they already had a small installed beta test base and leading computer makers had taken a small active interest in its development.

Unfortunately, there were significant bugs in the project. A research study suggested that the market wasn't ready for anything as advanced (and as expensive) as this executive desktop; suppliers of component parts were expressing their doubts that they could deliver on time and in budget. Whenever these and other pieces of bad news were brought before the CEO, he pooh-poohed them, as one vice president explained. He accused the messengers of bad news of having negative mind-sets and of being overly risk-averse. Pretty soon, no one wanted to tell the CEO anything negative about his pet project, and pretty soon, no one did.

At the retreat, the vice presidents resolved to confront the CEO on this subject, and the CEO, after some discussion and debate, agreed that he had a blind spot regarding this project and hired an outside consulting team to recommend whether to go forward or stop it. (They recommended stopping it.)

This "bad news" question, whether asked in its original format or flipped around, always raises a sensitive subject. No one likes to admit that they react badly to bad news or that they are afraid to tell it to others.

For this reason, many people answer this question with a comment like:

My people (or suppliers) feel free to tell me anything.

If you suspect this isn't the case, try asking the following question:

Do they feel free to tell you that they made a mistake that might result in a significant loss of time or money ..but also might not?

In other words, there's the possibility that the mistake might not result in something awful happening. At the same time, it would be much better if you knew about the potential for disaster so you could prepare for it. Whether you're the one not hearing the bad news or the one withholding it from someone else, this scenario sparks useful ideas and discussion.

66

You're the corporate weatherperson; what's your FORECAST for the ORGANIZATION (or department, team, individual career in company) using meteorological terms

FOUR GREAT WAYS TO USE THIS QUESTION

- Allows people to use weather forecasting terms to discuss business issues; there's a remarkable correspondence between the two.

- Gives people an opportunity to make predictions; helps people discover what they really think is going to happen to themselves and to other companies in the coming months.

- Demonstrates that just as no one can predict the weather, no one can foretell the fortunes of a company; also demonstrates how much fun it is to try.

- Helps shift the focus of a meeting from present problems to future possibilities.

We were with a sales team at their annual sales planning winter retreat. Though we were attempting to discuss problems and opportunities that might arise in the coming year, we kept returning to current sales figures and issues impacting those figures. To move everyone into the future, we asked the weather question.

Bad puns rained down upon us: "I predict a storm brewing in the area surrounding our largest customer"; "I forecast record highs if the low pressure zone in Competitorland stays to the north."

After a while, people became tired of their weather puns and examined the implications of what they were forecasting. Soon everyone was talking about problems and opportunities in the distance rather than those directly overhead.

USER'S MANUAL

Beware of silliness. Yes, the question invites some of this nonsense, but don't let the discussion get bogged down in it. The way to capitalize on this question is to get people thinking metereologically about the business. Here are some facilitating tips:

1. **Throw out some terms.** Ask the group to talk about the temperature, barometer, humidity, sky conditions, and potential storms. Suggest they use words such as fog, sun, fronts, low and high pressure, snow, wind, uncertain air mass, sudden drop, and so on.

2. **Ask them to give you their most optimistic forecast.** What conditions would be ideal for the company? How likely is it that those conditions will occur?

3. Suggest they forecast brutal weather. A flood of competitors, a new technology packing huge winds of change, a freeze on customer spending.

67

what are the TOP 10
reasons why your great
ideas fall apart during
IMPLEMENTATION **?**

- Opens a discussion of innovation and creativity processes.
- Sets up a lively debate between the people with the ideas and those assigned to implement them; helps both groups understand each other's issues and work to resolve them.

The marketing team of a financial services company was blasting the sales group for not having their act together. It was a year-end meeting, and the marketing manager was complaining, "It's time for sales to get their act together and start executing. We've initiated a half-dozen dynamite programs over the past year and sales just lets them sit there and fizzle out."

We asked our question and in the next hour we probably received more than our requested number of reasons:

They're lazy.

They don't care.

They're not sophisticated enough to understand what to do with our programs.

They start working on it and get bogged down in the details.

As they talked, the sales managers in the room gave their reasons:

Because their programs work in theory and not in practice.

They're not in touch with people in the field and don't understand what constraints we're working under.

They're dumb ideas.

We don't have enough time.

With "reasons" from both sides on the table, there was a basis for discussion. At first, it was more name-calling and scapegoating than discussion. But eventually it evolved to a higher level of communication in which both sides recognized that they were contributing to the implementation problem and needed to make changes.

Yes, this question does invite blaming. Don't try to stop it at first. Gobs of energy are released when we ask this question; people really have numerous reasons why it's someone else's fault that their terrific idea wasn't implemented properly.

Let people get the blaming out of their systems. Then ask them these follow-up questions to uncover the real issues:

- Is the failure responsibility totally someone else's fault or do you (or your group) accept some of the blame?
- Do you still feel the idea is as brilliant as when you originally came up with it?
- If you had the chance to relaunch the idea, what would you do differently?

If you can't move people from the blaming stage—if they insist on listing reason after reason why someone else screwed up—ask each person to discuss one reason in detail. If, for instance, someone says Joe's group screwed up the implementation because they didn't like the idea and sabotaged it, ask them if the group had a valid reason for its sabotage; have them talk about whether Joe's group has similarly destroyed other great ideas; wonder out loud if Joe is a self-destructive individual; ask if anyone in Joe's group might have been planted by a competitor to ruin the company. Taking a given reason to absurd conclusions often helps others think about whether their reason is valid.

If you could forge an ALLIANCE with any organization in THE WORLD to obtain a needed resource, which ONE would it be

FOUR GREAT WAYS TO USE THIS QUESTION

- Helps everyone in an organization develop a partnering mind-set; helps everyone from factory workers to top executives think in terms of alliances rather than "rugged individualism."

- Good strategic planning tool to identify the resources the company is missing.

- An ideal-to-real brainstorming device; you start out with the ideal partner and work your way toward a realistic choice.

- A tool to foster global thinking.

An old-line, low-tech midwestern manufacturing company convened a disparate group of employees to answer this question. We had everyone from an executive vice president to a secretary in the room. Before the meeting, we had talked with the company founder who said he expected that everyone would answer the question by naming a company in Japan that had world-class processes that would save them a great deal of money. While one person did name this company, the others chose a diverse group of companies with a diverse group of resources. What was interesting was that three of the people named Hallmark, saying that they wanted to learn how to operate a company profitably but with a great image and humanistic values. The three people claimed that their own company had an image problem: "We're viewed as cutthroat competitors and dictatorial in the way we treat our vendors. That was fine years ago, but it's a problem now— we've lost a number of customers who say our values don't match theirs." While the company didn't actually partner with Hallmark, they did make an effort to change their image (and the realities that shaped their old image).

This question is designed to fire the imagination. Reject expected, logical answers: "We want to partner with Company X because they have the expertise and technology we're missing." Encourage everyone to choose a "surprise" partner—a company that wouldn't occur to anyone at first. Remember, one of the uses of this question is to foster a partnering mind-set. People don't have to be top executives to come up with an answer. We had one line worker from a small metal stamping firm who told us he wanted to partner with the Leo Burnett ad agency so he could help his firm adopt their great benefits package.

To help people use their imagination with this question, suggest the following resources they might want to acquire:

- great leadership
- mind-blowing advertising
- top quality products
- wonderful publicity
- technology genius
- work environment alternatives (flexible hours, no dress code, etc.)

The ideal scenario for this question is to allow a lot of debate and discussion about the companies and resources named. If you're not getting this debate and discussion going, flip the question around. In other words, ask:

- What is the one company and resource you wouldn't partner with in a million years?

Sometimes the negative position produces hotter conversational sparks than the positive approach.

69

What would it be like to work for a company that is the exact opposite of the one you work for

TWO GREAT WAYS TO USE THIS QUESTION

- Helps people realize how lucky they are to work where they're working; the grass is always greener until you start examining the dirt beneath the grass.

- Enables everyone to consider an alternative to the status quo; offers an opportunity for employees to suggest changes that might improve the working environment.

WAR STORY

John's team was frustrated. They worked for a printing equipment manufacturer, and the team was focused on developing new business opportunities, but all their ideas had been shot down by management. The team requested a meeting with the CEO and two of his executives. During the meeting, John tried to convey how frustrated they were, citing the innovations made by a competitor and how difficult it was for them to do similarly innovative things.

The CEO began talking about all the advantages the team had and how that should translate into business opportunities. It struck John that the CEO really didn't grasp how many more advantages their competitor possessed. So he asked this "opposite" question.

The CEO and other team members talked about it, and everyone seemed to agree that their opposite would be a company that was service oriented, externally focused, and customer driven; they were a product-driven, nuts-and-bolts manufacturer. As the team described how rewarding it would be spending more time and money researching new markets and customers, the CEO got it. While he had no intention of turning the company into its opposite, he did relent a bit and gave the team a bigger research budget.

USER'S MANUAL

This is a versatile question. It can be used for everything from career development to corporate strategy. Most groups have little problem imagining what it would be like to work in a completely different environment. Most of them, in fact, tend to describe those opposite environments with great enthusiasm and longing.

The point of this question isn't to prove that the grass is always greener on the other side, but to help people view their own corporate environment in new ways. We've found that individuals come up with fresh ideas about their careers and company strategies and policies when they move beyond rhapsodizing about their opposites. The following questions will help you lead everyone to these fresh ideas:

- What do you think those who work for your opposite company would find attractive about your corporate environment?
- How would management defend your company's policies and programs against those of your opposite?
- Describe what your company considers the ideal employee; describe the opposite of that ideal; figure out where you and your team members fall between the two extremes.

If a **MAJOR** crisis along the lines of product tampering or a headline-making lawsuit were to strike your ORGANIZATION, what mistakes might MANAGEMENT make in dealing with the crisis?

THREE GREAT WAYS TO USE THIS QUESTION

- Reveals larger vulnerabilities; exposes areas of management that need to be strengthened, especially the decision-making process.

- Encourages nonmanagement people to think about crisis management; drives down the policy-making process to the rank and file who often are critical of dealing effectively with crises.

- Helps management anticipate errors they might make in a given scenario and plan accordingly.

WAR STORY

We were working with the executive staff of a company that had been spun off from a major pharmaceutical manufacturer. Though the purpose of this particular meeting was not crisis management, we were telling them the story of how we had used this question with another client and they immediately grew concerned. They had been so wrapped up in their first big product launch as an independent that they hadn't even considered crisis management issues—big issues in their industry. They all were very open to the idea of making mistakes in a crisis; they said they'd probably assume they had more resources than they really possessed. Unlike their former parent, they said they couldn't afford the large legal and public relations bills that such a crisis would precipitate. The discussion for the next two hours revolved around how they might manage a big crisis with a little budget.

USER'S MANUAL

You may find yourself confronted with blank stares when you ask this question. We've learned that if an organization hasn't been through a major crisis in its recent past—or if they're not in the type of business where crises are inevitable—they may consider the question a dry, intellectual exercise.

In this instance, you need to make the theoretical crisis real and immediate. One way to do this is to list potential crisis types and ask the group to suggest which type is most likely to occur (and then talk about the mistakes that might be made). Here are some common types:

- technological disaster (computer system crashes)
- lawsuit

- federal agency crackdown on deceptive or illegal practices
- environmental scandal
- severe financial problems
- product tampering

Another thing to remember about this question is that it works well with rank-and-file employees. They can offer insights about how the company might fail during a crisis; they may have observed that failure in the past. They also might have some good suggestions about how to deal with a crisis from a grassroots level.

Top management is wiped out by a tidal wave at their ANNUAL retreat in Bora Bora; when your team is put in charge of the company, how would you change things and who would be in charge **?**

FOUR GREAT WAYS TO USE THIS QUESTION

- This question is akin to fantasizing about being king or queen for a day; it gives nonmanagement people a chance to voice changes they feel would do the company good.

- A tool to evaluate management's performance; identifies what they're not doing that they should be doing.

- Helps people recognize the value and contributions of management; a natural discussion topic that emerges is what skills, leadership, and experience would be lost if top management departed.

- Provides a forum for addressing leadership issues within the team.

A group of middle managers at a fast-growing company responded to this question with the conspiratorial glee of a
group of soldiers planning to overthrow the government.
They admitted (reluctantly) that they might miss the significant experience and contacts of top managers, but they insisted that they would be able to change things for the better. At first, they all talked enthusiastically about how
they'd spend much more money in R&D because that's
where they felt they were being hurt by competitors; they
were also unanimous about wanting to push decision making down a level or two. But after about ten minutes, they
began disagreeing about other changes they'd make. Personal agendas surfaced. The women managers in the
group accused the men of ignoring glass ceiling issues.
And then they really came to blows over who should be in
charge. They bickered about who was the most qualified
person to lead the company and couldn't reach consensus.
By the end of the meeting, more than one person in the
group wondered wistfully if perhaps some of their management group had survived the tidal wave.

It's always easier to criticize than to solve problems. This
question works best when people come to realize that
management isn't as dumb, change-resistant, leaderless,
or indecisive as they appear; it's also great when the discussion veers onto topics such as how hard it is to make
change happen or to choose the right leader.

Sometimes discussions need to be nudged in these directions. It's easy for groups to just have fun speculating
about "if I were king." That's a good starting point, but

you want them to dig deeper for ideas about change and leadership. Here are some provocative ways to do so:

- Ask the group to name three things that they could do better than current management.

- Get them talking about what would be the biggest loss to the company in terms of skills, experience, leadership, ideas, etc. You might even want to have them identify the executive who the company could least afford to lose. Then ask them how they would plan to replace people and things.

- Encourage each of them to role play being CEO and talk about what they would do with that power.

How many STUPID, unproductive phone CONVERSATIONS do you have in the course of an AVERAGE workweek

THREE GREAT WAYS TO USE THIS QUESTION

- Everyone wastes a certain amount of time talking on the phone; this question quantifies the amount of time wasted.

- Helps people recognize that sometimes they talk too much and do too little.

- Catalyzes a discussion of time management.

WAR STORY

After a meeting in which we asked this question, an MIS manager decided to chart his stupid, unproductive phone calls during the following week. He then told us the results of his research. He'd received or made 89 business-related calls. Of those, he classified 74 of them as stupid and unproductive. He subdivided this group into "extraordinarily idiotic," "huge time-waster," and other categories. He found the stupidest, most time-consuming calls were ones he received from current suppliers who wanted to cover themselves because of some foul-up; the second worst were from people trying to sell him something; the third worst he described as going on what he called "information wild goose chases."

A few months later, this manager told us that just by being conscious of calls that were stupid, he was able to limit and to a certain extent control the time he spent talking on the phone.

USER'S MANUAL

Be prepared for a mixed bag of answers. Some people believe phone time is sacred and will challenge any charge that it's unproductive. Others will readily confess that they're guilty as charged and that 99 percent of their phone conversations are idiotic.

In both cases, the best way to make productive use of time spent discussing this issue is to ask for a specific description of typical phone conversations. When people volunteer the details of their calls—how long they lasted, who they were with, what the topic was—substantive issues emerge.

The ultimate goal of this question is to find break-through concepts for turning the phone into a productive communication tool. To solicit those concepts, here are some follow-up questions that will rattle cages and shake some good ideas loose:

- What would happen if you reduced the amount of time you talked to _____ by 50 percent?
- What are some reasonable excuses you might use to convince a caller that you have to get off the phone?
- How might you deal with issues that are wasting phone time by using other forms of communication (e-mail, fax, in-person meetings)?

If YOU CAN'T get people to address a serious problem through TRADITIONAL methods, what unusual or OUTRAGEOUS act might GET their attention?

THREE GREAT WAYS TO USE THIS QUESTION

- This is a "break-the-glass" fire alarm device; it helps companies identify neglected or ignored issues before they erupt.

- Demonstrates what really gets people to look and listen in organizations; facilitates a discussion of whether it's good or bad that the culture requires radical acts to get people's attention.

- A catalyst for creative and out-of-the-box thinking about problems facing teams, departments, and companies.

A work team got together and was grousing about the reporting process. One member complained that the time reports were demeaning; another said that they contradicted what the company preached about trusting its workers to hold themselves accountable rather than fearing Big Brother. Our question produced a number of amusing and suitably outrageous ideas, but the one that captured everyone's attention was the suggestion to "introduce a computer virus that would knock out the whole time system." Energized by the idea, the team members mapped out how it would be possible to create such a virus and speculated on how the destruction of the system would lift morale.

We're not sure whether the reporting process was modified because management finally recognized that it was in need of modification or because they feared the virus the team claimed it could create.

USER'S MANUAL

Responses will fall into the following three categories:

- **Funny.** "I'm going to come to work dressed like a bum, march into my boss' office, and demand he listen to my request for a raise so I can at least afford a few new suits."

- **Angry.** "I'm going to cause a scene in the office; maybe that will convince people here that we've got a problem."

- **Strategic.** "I'm going to send memos to every manager who has ever sent me one about the need for five additional meaningless memos per week."

It's fine to let people suggest the first two, but the most productive discussion will come out of outrageous strategic suggestions. They are more thoughtful than the others and lead to more thoughtful discussions of problems and ways to snag people's attention. The other two just lead to laughter and resentment.

74

What particular accomplishment or failure might cause you or your organization to make HEADLINES in Business Week magazine?

TWO GREAT WAYS TO USE THIS QUESTION

- Helps everyone think big; rouses employees out of their safe and conservative mind-sets and encourages them to contribute ambitious, unusual, and outrageous ideas.

- Helps people think about consequences; gets them to anticipate the downside of ideas with a potentially big upside.

WAR STORY

"About the only thing that would get us a headline, at least a positive one, would be if we made a major acquisition." This comment was made in an offhand way by a supervisor who worked for a large but dull accounting firm. In response to our question, there was a lot of grumbling about the fact that the firm never did anything significant (though they joked that it was more likely that they might get negative headlines if the media found out about some of their accounting practices). The offhanded comment about the acquisition didn't generate much interest—at first. But after we got past the unlikeliness of it occurring, people were willing to speculate about the possibility. The general consensus was that it would not only make headlines, but it would be great for the firm—they desperately needed the synergy of a merger or acquisition, something to fuel expansion into fresh markets. Two years later, this firm did merge with another accounting firm, made the headlines, and the new entity has been growing like crazy. Though we don't claim credit for this happening, we like to think that our cage-rattling question helped shake loose the idea of a merger in at least a few minds.

USER'S MANUAL

This question usually works pretty well on its own. People enjoy speculating about incredible successes and abysmal failures. We've had people tell us corporate secrets, individual dreams, and very real fears that would yield headlines. Sometimes those fears have to do with bankruptcy or downsizing; the hopes and dreams often have to do with new products or innovative processes and policies.

Still, sometimes people get stuck and can't imagine what an appropriate answer would be. Here's a simple trick to get them (or yourself) unstuck. Look at some business publications and read the headlines. You'll find things like:

Cloak and Dagger in the Industry! Company A's consumer unit engaged in blatant espionage, Attorney General claims.

Stock Soars As Company Q Introduces New Product.

Company G Takes Fresh Approach to Customer Complaints.

Company B Cleans House. A squeaky-clean company places itself on risky legal ground by sudden exposure of sexual harassment.

Monkey Business in Technology Land? Company D may be the focus in an FTC probe of customer billing practices.

Company Y Names First Woman CEO.

If these headlines don't catalyze thought and discussion, try the following fill-in-the-blank exercise. Once people fill them in, headlines come naturally:

What led _____ to propose huge _____, offset only by vague plans to _____?

_____ (your name) discovers _____; industry abuzz over innovative _____.

_____ is starting to worry about how _____ will _____ and affect _____.

_____ (your name) is subject of intensive search, having taken _____ and left the country.

_____ is embracing a new _____. Customers could end up benefiting by _____ and more _____.

A growing _____ against _____ reform is stalling the _____ agenda. _____ won't do much to pick up the pace.

Don't be surprised if _____ races ahead in _____, and (your group) ends up _____. As usual, they _____ more _____.

While _____ scrambles for _____ … _____ is angling for _____ to maintain _____.

75

What QUESTION might you create to rattle the cages of PEOPLE you work with (including yourself)

THREE GREAT WAYS TO USE THIS QUESTION

- Gives people the chance to adapt these cage-rattling questions to specific problems and opportunities in their work environments.

- It scratches an itch; all of us have the mischievous impulse to rattle some cages now and then.

- Allows people to practice asking before they act; gets them into the habit of asking tough questions *before* problems happen.

WAR STORY

A mid-sized button manufacturer had been in business for almost 100 years. During a long-range planning meeting of the company's executives, we put this question to them and this is what one of them came up with:

Why is this company still in business?

Sometimes cage-rattling questions evoke a lot of noise. This one produced a profound silence. Profound because everyone in that room was trying to come to grips with the fact that the company really had no justifiable reason for still existing. The number of low-cost button manufacturers had grown enormously in recent years, taking away a lot of their customers. There were also companies out there that had superior design and manufacturing capabilities to produce higher-quality buttons. The company was left with a rapidly shrinking middle market. Still, that market remained profitable because of the loyalty of some key long-term customers. This question verbalized what had been on everyone's minds—What happens when we lose those customers? Where is our market?

By bringing the issue into the open, the staff was able to start working on a strategy for developing new niche-oriented products and finding new markets.

USER'S MANUAL

Our best piece of advice regarding this final question: Accept no dull, uninspired, or otherwise routine questions. Some people's idea of a cage-rattler may be to ask, "Have we done everything we can do to make this a good year?" You want questions that touch a nerve, that push the imagination envelope, that make people think in new and unexpected directions.

Communicate that point to a group. Give them a list of questions that will be unacceptable, such as:

- What can we do better?
- What three things can we do to communicate better?
- How can each of us contribute to increase the company's productivity and profitability?

Emphasize the importance of being specific and provocative rather than general and mundane. One technique you might find useful is to ask a group to come up with a list of these questions and have them discuss and debate them until they agree on the one that really rattles their cages.

About the Authors

Dick Whitney is a market development specialist with Mercer Management Consulting. His clients have ranged from start-ups to global leaders.

Melissa Giovagnoli is the president of Service Showcase, Inc., an eleven-year-old consulting and training firm specializing in team building and retreat planning using the Cage Rattling *Questioneering* Process.